"Author Roger Darnell does an excellent job breaking down a complex subject in the pages of his book, *The Communications Consultant's Foundation*. I would highly recommend the book for students and professionals, as this handy reference guide is rich with helpful information that's focused on building a communications consulting business and achieving greater success along the way."

—Deirdre Breakenridge, CEO of Pure Performance, speaker, author

"Roger has written a true field guide for communications consulting, covering everything from branding to business development and finances. An excellent read filled with practical advice for any enterprising professional who dreams of becoming a trusted advisor."

—Elise Mitchell, Principal, Velocity Collective and elisemitchell.com

"A must-read for rising PR professionals. As with the best business books, Mr. Darnell frames the PR business as a calling, one with a set of principles and a way to contextualize concepts with real-life examples. Being great at something literally comes down to understanding the abstraction levels of that practice. This book helps readers achieve that."

—Ric Peralta, Founder, RogueID, former Chairman and CEO, ATTIK

"This informative and compelling narrative from an accomplished public relations and marketing expert guides and inspires all those interested in liberating their careers in the 21st century post-COVID. Blending astute research and vast empirical knowledge, this book prepares readers to navigate the world as dynamic, successful, independent communications consultants."

—Dean Ramser, Ed.D.

"Roger Darnell is a best-in-class PR expert with legacy experience that provides a diverse playbook capable of accommodating anything that could arise in a company, especially a creative company where the lines blur a bit. I am so pleased Roger has penned this book. Having worked with him for many years now I have benefited from his experience and distinct point-of-view… and now you can, too!"

—Erin Sarofsky, Executive Creative Director & Owner, Sarofsky Corp.

"Roger Darnell's expertise and services have been key to Leviathan's success over the last decade. To have all of his public relations knowledge packed into a concise compendium such as *The Communications Consultant's Foundation* is a tremendous value."

—Chad Hutson, CEO, Leviathan

"Ethics and strategic communications are going to be of the utmost importance in the next decade for great leadership. Roger goes well beyond the foundations to show you how to aim and succeed in this new book."

—George Hedon, Enabler of Awesome, Pause Fest

"Roger Darnell's guidance was crucial during the acquisition of my first feature film. Whether you are interested in a career in communications or like me, looking to gain tangible PR strategies to get to where you want to go in your profession, I highly recommend this book!"

—Finnerty Steeves, Actor/Writer/Producer, Marsha's Daughter Productions

"Roger has done it again. A master class in vital skills that will set you up for success. Even seasoned professionals will learn valuable lessons and benefit from this expert advice."

—Shelly Palmer, Business advisor, author, commentator

"Excellent read for both the student and the client. My three top takeaways: Aim high, ethics count, and be sure there is truth in your storytelling."

—Pamela Tuscany, Vice President and General Manager, Universal Studios Florida Production Group

"Roger's invaluable insight extends way beyond simply writing a good press release. His deep understanding of the creative industry informs his methodical, holistic approach to reputation management."

—Adam Gault, Partner, BLOCK & TACKLE

"Roger Darnell is a class-act and master of his craft in Public Relations. From my first interaction with Roger, it was obvious he trail-blazed his path to representing some of the top names in the creative industry by putting respect at the forefront and implementing a considered demeanor that kindles the prized trust. In this book, Roger generously shares his tried-and-true methods and packs each page with personal anecdotes, well-researched insights from other visionaries in the field, and offers thorough exercises so you too can hone your skill set and become a successful, independent, and sought-after PR whiz."

—Bevin McNamara, Filmmaker, Creative Director, former Editor-in-Chief, Motionographer.com

The Communications Consultant's Foundation

For all professionals and students who want to improve their prospects in business, this book prepares and positions them to build dream careers, giving them the education and guidance required to develop vital soft skills, and work remotely and independently.

After establishing a foundation for solid professional communications on a personal level, it quickly opens doors to business insights and opportunities that are exciting, inspiring, and highly sustainable. Immersing readers into the key realms of business success and exploring the full spectrum of essential communications practices, they gain knowledge and trade skills of immense value, including:

- The basics of positive, proactive, strategic communications for individuals and organizations
- What it means to be a PR expert in the creative industry and to do great work
- An introduction to essential business imperatives, with high-level instruction on creativity, strategy, leadership, management, marketing, and much more
- Customer service and all it entails
- Extensive exploration of the PR toolset and its application in real-world marketing scenarios

This book brings home all instruction with sophisticated questions and challenges, ensuring readers have every opportunity to comprehend and grow, step by step.

Roger Darnell is an author, communications consultant, publisher, and speaker. Already central to billions of positive media impressions worldwide, his ambitious collaborations with entrepreneurs and media luminaries continue soaring to new heights.

The Communications Consultant's Foundation

Leveraging Public Relations Expertise for Personal and Client Success

Roger Darnell

NEW YORK AND LONDON

First published 2022
by Routledge
605 Third Avenue, New York, NY 10158

and by Routledge
2 Park Square, Milton Park, Abingdon, Oxon, OX14 4RN

Routledge is an imprint of the Taylor & Francis Group, an informa business

© 2022 Roger Darnell

The right of Roger Darnell to be identified as author of this work has been asserted by him in accordance with sections 77 and 78 of the Copyright, Designs and Patents Act 1988.

All rights reserved. No part of this book may be reprinted or reproduced or utilised in any form or by any electronic, mechanical, or other means, now known or hereafter invented, including photocopying and recording, or in any information storage or retrieval system, without permission in writing from the publishers.

Trademark notice: Product or corporate names may be trademarks or registered trademarks, and are used only for identification and explanation without intent to infringe.

Library of Congress Cataloging-in-Publication Data
Names: Darnell, Roger, author.
Title: The communications consultant's foundation : leveraging public relations expertise for personal and client success / Roger Darnell.
Description: New York, NY : Routledge, 2022. | Includes bibliographical references and index.
Identifiers: LCCN 2021012835 (print) | LCCN 2021012836 (ebook) | ISBN 9781032012650 (hardback) | ISBN 9781032012674 (paperback) | ISBN 9781003177951 (ebook)
Subjects: LCSH: Public relations consultants—Handbooks, manuals, etc. | Public relations—Vocational guidance.
Classification: LCC HD59 .D256 2022 (print) | LCC HD59 (ebook) | DDC 659.2023—dc23
LC record available at https://lccn.loc.gov/2021012835
LC ebook record available at https://lccn.loc.gov/2021012836

ISBN: 9781032012650 (hbk)
ISBN: 9781032012674 (pbk)
ISBN: 9781003177951 (ebk)

DOI: 10.4324/9781003177951

Typeset in Goudy
by codeMantra

For all those willing to work hard, where encouragement can lighten the load, and inside knowledge can revolutionize the world.

Dedicated to my better half Beth, our wonderful family members and friends, and to all the illustrious clients of The Darnell Works Agency, past and present.

Contents

List of Figures		xi
List of Tables		xii
i	Introduction	1
ii	My Story	6
Part I	**Foundations**	**9**
1	Reputation Management and Ethics	11
2	Creativity	19
3	Strategy	24
4	Personal Brands and Branding	30
Part II	**The Arena**	**47**
5	Leadership and Management	49
6	Objectives	59
7	Business Brands and Branding	67
8	Business Development	80
9	Customer Service	89
10	Integrated Marketing in Action	97
11	Cash Flow and Project Flow	107

Contents

Part III Communications Consulting — 117

12 The Communications Consultant in Practice — 119
13 Consistencies and Variations by Client Size — 129
14 Media and Its Usage — 140
15 My Version and Your Version — 151
16 Is Consulting Right for You? — 156

Index — 169

Figures

1	The ADDIE Instructional Design Model	33
2	Greiner's Model Curve	56
3	Six Components of Human Beings	90
4	Campaign Messaging Plan	113
5	Roles and Responsibilities of the PR Champion	123
6	Social Media Strategy and Tactics	124
7	Happiness at Work	157

Tables

1	Personal Brand Analysis	34
2	The Copy Platform	36
3	Brands by ATTIK	73
4	Small Company Consistencies and Variations	133
5	Medium-Sized Company Consistencies and Variations	135
6	Bigger Company Consistencies and Variations	137

i
Introduction

Whether we like it or not, we all eventually must get a job. Even as toddlers, we are asked what we want to be when we grow up. Despite so much prep time, finding one's ideal vocation can still be a harrowing experience, as I have learned.

My own toughest time trying to earn a living came right after graduating from high school. It primarily involved a fevered devotion to my local newspaper's classified ads. Thinking back to those days, measuring myself up against one meticulous short description after another, where I simply hoped to locate a fitting chance to trade work for good wages, I can still recall the dread and panic.

Thankfully, after gaining more education and experience, the hunts started to become more rewarding. Recalling the improved situations, I realize I had prepared for them with a lot of effort, including the training and education I gained along the way. Today, my confidence in communication builds on all that diligence and training, and each opportunity I have seized to learn, grow, apply, and prove myself.

In my work as a communications consultant, I see all the ways people with my skill set create value for others. Even during global pandemics, there are individuals and businesses that need people like us to consistently focus on applying solid promotional communications principles on their behalf. By combining intelligent strategic thinking with such focused effort, and doing good work, I am sure you can seize similar opportunities to succeed in business. Adjusting the strategies and tactics deftly, applying solid management and customer service efforts can sustain the productivity of your relationships, and continually increase mutual success.

Introduction

This is the true story of the past and present of my professional transformation, and the future of yours.

*

Whenever I speak with someone facing a career challenge, I begin thinking how I can help them understand my approach to the subject, the ways I view opportunities and the specific types of arrangements I envision that can help them earn above-average wages without necessarily being full-time employees. Working as part of a company's staff is something I do highly recommend whenever it feels like the right fit. For short spans during my teens, 20s and 30s, I was pressed into different employment and volunteer scenarios. Fortunately, I could usually earn about U.S. $10 per hour. With at least 25 of those hours in a week, and one U.S. Air Force Reserve weekend per month, that is how I paid my bills, earned a couple of college degrees, and got my career moving upward.

While there are full- and part-time staff positions, there are also freelance (or contract) opportunities. Even before college graduation, I began building my career using that latter approach. Since age 22, I have been self-employed for all but 27 months. Compared with the way most people work, this represents a different, more independent way of earning money, but it also requires planning, dedication, and discipline that goes well beyond an hourly wage. To me, the long-term financial prospects of independent contracting far outweigh the unique commitments, especially when you consider how employable you can become, and how freely you can live, when you learn the ropes.

My goal in creating this curriculum is to help you learn what I know about handling strategic and promotional communications services. Whether you use this knowledge as an employee or as an independent contractor is entirely up to you. With my guidance, I am confident you can become an astute communications practitioner, with skills and approaches that allow you to earn excellent wages consistently, meaningfully.

Part 1: Foundations

There are certain hallmarks of intelligent communications that stand out from history. We can harvest the lessons of many great, enterprising people who have established platforms for savvy communications practices.

Understanding the reach and the tenets of reputations, and the role of ethics, offers a viable basis for earning and maintaining respect.

Next, gaining a true understanding of what Creativity means to those who excel in the creative industry is eye- opening. Taking their outlooks and practices to heart will allow you to use problem-solving as an uplifting, highly fulfilling, and extremely valuable routine exercise.

Strategy is another tried-and-true means for focusing efforts to ensure they are effective. Assessing my own career trajectory, and emphasizing some of the more impactful transitions, can help you streamline your ascent.

In business communications, the building blocks for brands include names, symbols, positioning statements, color schemes, and other strategic elements. As surely as we live and breathe, each of us represents our own personal brand. Finding the most apt meaning for yours – and translating it powerfully to help you fulfill your aims – is a thrilling mission we will complete together.

Part 2: The Arena

This section widens our outlook to examine the pillars of business success. Its goal is to provide enough of a core foundation in areas including leadership and management to allow you to quickly identify the strengths and weaknesses of those you may choose to work with. The ability to identify good leaders and organizations can help you ensure you are giving yourself the best opportunities to succeed and be part of winning teams.

The importance of your personal objectives, and the operational objectives of your clients, cannot be overstated. Few organizations exist that do not need to continuously optimize employee activities to meet their bottom lines, especially when difficulties arise. Clarifying these imperatives, and focusing on fulfilling them intelligently, is absolutely mission-critical.

The brand at the heart of any business carries meaning that is reflected in every nuance of its existence, including the behavior of its employees. Communications initiatives also must pass the test of staying "on brand." There is much to know about stellar brand communications, as you will learn.

Speaking of mission-critical imperatives, no business can succeed for long without sales and attentive customer service. Drawing on expert knowledge, these and other core aspects of smart companies – including integrated marketing, profitability, and project management – are broken down to essentials, and illuminated as parts of our playbook for success.

Part 3: Communications Consulting

This curriculum allows you to engage with an accomplished communications practitioner, as some intense experiences are put in the spotlight, then analyzed according to the job's key skill set and other particulars. This vocation can vary greatly, according to the size of the client company, for starters. This in-depth examination draws on more than 20 years of high-pressure campaigns, serving up invaluable tips and insights.

With the ubiquity of cell phones and smart devices, the amount of content we can consume at the swipe of our fingers is infinite. Those who act as creators and curators know how the handling of media must be managed to achieve certain objectives (including getting 'likes'). This book's chapter on Media and its Usage explores such details from the POV of corporate storytelling, and media-relations.

By investigating these aspects of a communications practitioner's exploits, the applications spring to life. Assessing those details and surveying other leading PR practitioners provides more unique vantage points from which to assess your interest in this burgeoning, rewarding career field.

Completing this journey's foundation, a more thorough examination of the most important factors involved in non-employee work scenarios will help you begin considering whether consulting is right for you. Will you take the plunge right away – or first seek to gain more specific work experience through an employer?

Prepare to Embark

If it is not already clear, I will be sharing many first-hand life experiences, to activate your internal problem-solver and help render lessons and key points. As mentioned, the primary objective for this book is teaching you what I have learned. By studying what I have faced and achieved in the field, you can fully comprehend the rewards and pitfalls, and blaze a unique, highly rewarding career path. The resulting capabilities can absolutely transform your existence.

Please also give extra special attention to the exercises concluding each chapter. To seize the greatest rewards, give each Exploration section great care and attention: This is where your journey advances.

Exploration

1. Complete this sentence and fill-in the author's name (if it does not sound familiar, Google it). "Choose a job you love, and you will never have _____ _____ _____ _____ _____ _____ _____." Who is the author (and are you sure about that)?
2. List three men and three women you know with untraditional jobs and describe their jobs.
3. Name five people who have dream jobs, from your point of view.
4. How much money are you worth per hour, when you are doing your absolute best work – and why are you worth that much?
5. What job would you hate to have?
6. If you could have a job doing anything for another person or company, what would it be?
7. Using seven words or less, write a new slogan for an advertising campaign for a favorite brand.
8. Find and watch a TED Talk that has to do with creativity.
9. What event in history would you like to be able to attend, and why?
10. What could you talk about in a TED Talk of your own – either now or in several years when your career has taken off?

ii
My Story

It is a great honor for me to lead you on this voyage of self-discovery and specialized business education, based on a career trajectory that has been extremely fun and rewarding. Not so long ago, I was starting out, and since then, I have learned that every person and opportunity met along the way can absolutely transform the world. Since we are still strangers, here is a quick tour of some of the experiences illuminated in this book, to help light the way for you.

As a high school student, I had earned good grades and demonstrated enough aptitude that college seemed like a sure thing. I gambled on winning a four-year Air Force Reserve Officer Training Corps scholarship that did not materialize, and found myself entering the workforce with no clear pathway forward. Still, the Air Force's powerful campaign urging everyone to "Aim High" pulled me in; as a Reservist, I got the leg up I needed to begin studying at the University of Central Florida.

By the time I graduated from UCF, I was intent on using the positive feedback I had earned as a writer to make my mark in the world of motion pictures. Two amazing openings occurred right away. First, as a VIP tour guide for the grand opening of Universal Studios Florida (USF), I was briefly allowed to step into the world of Hollywood moguls and celebrities. I also earned a part-time job writing press releases for the impressive post-production business Century III, which made its home at USF.

Despite my persistence, the results from my efforts to land more hands-on employment in "the industry" were up and down. So, I applied myself freelancing – including word-processing work for defense contractors – and eventually, using the writing and photojournalist skills I had sharpened through my Air Force Reserve training, I started placing some nonfiction articles in trade publications. I also submitted a lot of creative writing to prominent literary reviews, scoring a few placements and starting to understand what it meant to succeed – and get paid – as a professional writer.

With experience and determination, better prospects began arising. While the scripts I wrote for major sales conferences and cruise lines paid the bills, it was my technical writing skills – and my interest in film – that opened the most exciting doors. Between 1994 and 1997, I found work as a network TV script coordinator. That momentum led my wife and me to relocate to Los Angeles.

Despite my hopes for screenwriting my way to success, even with lots of connections at the top of both the feature film and TV industries, all of that came up short. This ultimately led to 24 months of employment in LA, representing an education unto itself. It was the Century III experience, and my success writing articles for industry trade publications, that helped me land my first job in LA. From there, I was the director of marketing for a creative production company in the promo space, which led to a career-opening position as an account executive for a high-tech focused PR firm, The Terpin Group (TTG).

At that point, I was no longer pining away for a career in the movies, for a few key reasons. I had learned that the production industry demands most of one's time – 14-hour days and six-day work weeks are standard. Being part of the crew on TV series for FOX, NBC and HBO taught me a lot about my work preferences. At TTG, I earned good money working regular hours … but I also saw the difference between what the agency billed, and what I was paid. So, after learning all the PR agency ropes over the span of about seven months, I was able to launch The Darnell Works Agency (DWA) and immediately double my income, while working from home.

This was an amazing turn of events for me. Once again, it became extra meaningful due to my focus on film and TV, and the people in my life at that time. One of my colleagues at TTG recommended me for an account she had previously handled. This became my first account in the commercial advertising industry. The client group was extraordinary, and it was essential in demonstrating my capabilities at the highest level. In other words, it was a perfect fit, and it set me on the path of independent success.

Within a year of launching DWA, my wife and I made another big move, leaving LA for the mountains of North Carolina, and starting a family. At the time of our departure, my business was thriving. What would be the impact of leaving that dream factory, for a small college town in the Appalachian Mountains? In short, we have come through several massive economic downturns, the unmeasurable upheaval of 9/11, and a global pandemic, in excellent shape.

At the beginning of my career journey, finding work was not easy. It was certain to require me going to work at some location, doing my job according to a schedule set by my boss, and hoping that things would go well, that I would have some job security, and maybe eventually, some perks. The dreams of working from home, living where I chose, earning over U.S. $100 per hour, and being able to pick and choose clients, were beyond my reach. How in the world could I ever make them a reality?

This book is here to achieve just that. If you have similar aspirations, read on. With diligence, we are going to elevate your journey.

Part 1

Foundations

Topics Covered

Reputation Management and Ethics   11
Creativity   19
Strategy   24
Personal Brands and Branding   30

1
Reputation Management and Ethics

When I was a bright-eyed 17-year-old, I had some extremely ambitious career aspirations; they were all summarized brilliantly by the United States Air Force's world-famous slogan: Aim High.

That is just one of many good reasons for selecting reputation management as the first topic in this book. Time and again, executives from different companies – and even different countries – tell me that a main goal of their new PR program is to ensure that the company's reputation precedes it. Of course, none of them were talking about any of the negative buzz, like gossip from their holiday party or the mixed reviews posted on their Facebook pages; they were exclusively wanting to spotlight their best work, their grandest accolades, their charitable activities … and imagining future business meetings where every attendee would already possess a solid understanding of the company's strengths, capabilities, and the most positive aspects of its character. To be clear, when they talk about their "reputations," they only mean *all the good stuff*.

Like most other consumers, even when I am wearing my hat as a communications consultant, I look at many aspects of a company to get a sense of its reputation. Certainly, if something bad is known to have happened in the past, that is absolutely one of the key ingredients … and that is never easy to offset. In fact, there are many PR firms specializing in handling exactly that type of situation, well known as "crisis communications." Even startups are responsible for telling their own stories well. Most people expect to be able to research a company and assess it quickly and accurately. If one is to be rewarded with our money, it must pass our tests for shared values.

Every area that contributes to a company's reputation can benefit from proactive communications efforts to educate the world and potentially shape perceptions. We all know that bad news travels fast, and history shows that

DOI: 10.4324/9781003177951-1

overcoming negativity requires many elements ... generally including taking responsibility, making and sustaining corrective efforts in good faith, and sticking to the corrected course over time.

These points underscore a fact many take for granted: Companies and individuals require positive reputations to succeed. In the corporate world, recent studies place the value of good reputations even higher than lines of bank credit.[1] The Harris Poll Reputation Quotient elegantly illuminates the many factors that make up a company's reputation by identifying these six dimensions: social responsibility; emotional appeal; products and services; workplace environment; financial performance; and vision and leadership.[2] Reputation management is the process we employ to ensure that people will think about companies and people the way they wish to be perceived.

The Anatomy of an Influencer

Dale Carnegie's book *How to Win Friends and Influence People* first appeared in 1936, and it was based on a 14-week course taught by Mr. Carnegie himself, which aimed to help individuals put themselves on the right track toward success. Whatever is implied by the expression "straighten up and fly right" seems to fit with the model behavior Mr. Carnegie taught others in his methodical approaches toward becoming reputable.

Designing this curriculum involved a great deal of analysis regarding my mission and responsibilities as a communications consultant. Across the successes, one specific piece of feedback reflects a daily internal focus which has ultimately paid massive dividends. In the words of creative director, director, and photographer Justin Meredith, "One of Roger's defining characteristics is keeping both internal and external communication positive."

With that in mind, my attraction to Mr. Carnegie's optimism-in-action is easy to see. To absorb the discussions to come, I feel one should embrace the basic tenets of professional etiquette and be able to apply them personally. Further, to me, the ability to remain positive in all situations is mandatory for anyone seeking to manage reputations for others.

Each of the discussions to follow is built on a foundation of personal conduct that is essentially impeccable, and of undeniable integrity. By successfully taking this training to heart, you will be in the position to offer excellent counsel to any business executive on any subject where you have established your expertise.

Mr. Carnegie spent 14 weeks bringing his students to the point of being solid, interesting, influential people. If you have never been exposed to good leadership, I encourage you to read *How to Win Friends and Influence People in the Digital Age*, as well as career guidance workbooks like *What Color is Your Parachute*, and to have enough conversations with smart, positive, respectable people about yourself, to have a good grasp of these two things:

- You are proud of yourself.
- You are willing to take on a proactive role to communicate with the world.

This emphasis on professional personal conduct directly addresses the fact that many people think of public relations as reputation management. To be fit for such service, one must measure up to very high standards.

Commitments to the Audience

In the advertising industry, the debut of the annual AICP Show in New York City is always a big deal, drawing attendance from agency executives and the Who's Who of commercial production professionals worldwide. Attending one year, I met an executive for a massive ad agency, where I had often engaged with his VP of Public Relations, and knew him to be quirky but friendly. When I asked if the PR VP was in attendance, my question immediately caused him to bristle. "He's not the kind of guy I typically hang out with," was the reply. To me, that represented another level of proficiency to aim for.

Although this standard may be impossible to meet, I take it as my *challenge* to be the type of person people will be happy to associate with. With the increasing difficulty of gaining attention, this subjective aspiration remains a benchmark for me. Being at least worthy of someone's time – in a word, interesting – puts the right emphasis on what the job of a communications consultant entails, at least to me. To summarize:

- Being a good communications consultant means interacting effectively with others and making that process as interesting as possible for them.

I will offer two more pearls of wisdom here. The first comes from author and former presidential speechwriter James Humes: "The art of communication is the language of leadership."[3]

And distilling some of Mr. Carnegie's teachings, taking interest in others may be the best way to earn their esteem.

I also have strong feelings about having a personal mission and pursuing it diligently over time, which is a main reason this book exists. Feeding one's personal development through ongoing education, and by challenging oneself to grow, are vital in becoming someone worth knowing.

The importance of staying informed about others and making efforts to understand their cares and concerns (especially those affecting the workplace) cannot be overemphasized. Communications are all about the audience; as we devise strategies and translate them into action, we attempt to drive certain responses. Only by being well versed in others' mindsets, motivations, and particulars can we hope to be successful as communicators.

Helping a Business Take Aim

Understanding the basic meaning of a business reputation, and considering what goes into managing one, it is easy to see the power of the world-class skill set at the heart of this book. The next part of the equation is about strategy.

If you have any experience working for a small business, no matter what your job was, you probably have some sense of the source of the cash-flow, or how the money came in. In the big picture, a main strategy for any professional or business is typically aimed at helping to support cash-flow, which usually comes down to sales, fundraising, underwriting and/or deal-making. Well-managed brands with long-term vision and deeper resources engage in brand-building and – in the best cases – socially responsible campaigns, knowing that their fortunes generally rely on positive reputations. And in the beginning stages, most businesses must start with a name, business cards, directory listings, often a website ... because without them, they have no credibility. By defining the bottom-line objectives for a business, (for example, (1) try to attract new customers; (2) take excellent care of existing customers so they will continue to buy from us), you can then start to understand what their strategy should be. We will be covering all of this in more depth, but I wanted to highlight strategy's essential role before talking about another key aspect of communication, which has to do with discerning right from wrong.

Ethics

I was retained by global creative agency ATTIK in 2003 to serve as its PR agency of record. For my small business, it was one of several prestigious accounts that motivated me to be among the best PR consultants in the creative industry. Over the next couple of years, I can think of very few scenarios which put me on the spot regarding my values, making me question whether I wanted to take on an assignment ... but there was one.

During that era, ATTIK's UK office was retained by Japan Tobacco, Inc. to rebrand and reposition its Camel brand of cigarettes, aiming to optimize its brand perception worldwide. When I was being briefed on the idea of trying to generate some media coverage through a PR campaign focusing on ATTIK's work, I was surprised at how the conversations struck my nerves, producing some negative sensations. Could I tell my client that this was a project I did not want to touch? My solution was to provide an action plan to frame up the strategy and proposed tactics, but I made it clear to my boss that I would prefer not to pitch it to the media, and I did not want my name attached to it.

In another instance, I was hired by the owner of a production company to help him generate media exposure around a project he had produced, which was about to win an award. I wrote the story according to his specifications, but when I told him we needed to get client approval, imagine my surprise when he told me, point blank: "Fuck them!" Based on my experience working in the creative industry, I let him know that I was uncomfortable distributing a story to a trade media outlet that tells only one side of a story, does not give everyone involved due credit, or may be inaccurate. Unmoved by my insistence that forging ahead distributing that story without the main client's input and approval would be a bad idea – I told them it would be like giving a journalist a gun that we were likely to get shot with – I ultimately refused to proceed, and refunded their money. While that was a difficult situation, it was also an important moment, teaching me how much it is worth to protect my reputation.

The late American Supreme Court Justice Potter Stewart once made this profound point: You may have a right to do something, but is it right to do it? Ethics is understanding the difference.[4] For your further reference as you navigate these waters, we can point to some widely respected ethical guidelines that serve bright human beings and professionals each day. Especially in a democracy like America, one can get the idea that right and wrong are indistinct. The standards we are about to discuss help us assess the ethics involved in situations we confront, and define the moral implications, so we can better sort right from wrong – good potential impacts to our reputations from bad ones – and handle decisions accordingly.

Ethics in Life

Over the past century, the Girl Scouts of the USA and Boy Scouts of America organizations have guided the lives of well over 60 million girls and young women, and 100 million boys and young men. The oaths each has voluntarily agreed to abide by bear strong similarities. Here are the Boy Scouts' vows.

- On my honor, I will do my best to do my duty to God and my country and to obey the Scout Law; to help other people at all times; to keep myself physically strong, mentally awake and morally straight.[5]
    - Law: A Scout is Trustworthy, Loyal, Helpful, Friendly, Courteous, Kind, Obedient, Cheerful, Thrifty, Brave, Clean, and Reverent.

Also worth noting, both Girl Scouts and Boy Scouts are committed to doing a good turn daily.

Ethics in Business

Many professional fields have adopted oaths that define the ethical standards its practitioners vow to uphold. The Hippocratic Oath[6] has been around for thousands of years now, and to this day, it represents a set of ideas we all can expect medical doctors to honor.

Among the multitude of avenues leading to business leadership, the one chosen by those who attend Harvard Business School's Masters in Business Administration (MBA) program is tried and true. A group of 2009 graduates decided to formulate its own oath, drawing inspiration from others, like this one from the Thunderbird School of Global Management at Arizona State University.[7]

- As a Thunderbird and a global citizen, I promise: I will strive to act with honesty and integrity, I will respect the rights and dignity of all people, I will strive to create sustainable prosperity worldwide, I will oppose all forms of corruption and exploitation, and I will take responsibility for my actions. As I hold true to these principles, it is my hope that I may enjoy an honorable reputation and peace of conscience. This pledge I make freely and upon my honor.

Just as Thunderbird graduates unite to speak these words at their commencement ceremony, and rising medical doctors engage in similar group activities which bind their individual decisions to common ideals judged to be good and necessary, the authors of the MBA Oath invite anyone to use their website to voluntarily pledge to being ethical and responsible. The website is http://www.mbaoath.org.

Through the stories I shared where I mentioned getting negative sensations, and even deciding that my only course of action was to refund payment and walk away, it is clear that communications consultants have important roles, just like MBA graduates and doctors. Without doubt, we must prepare to field requests where doing so may very well jeopardize our personal or our clients' reputations, and bottom-line success. Aiming for and maintaining unquestionable standards of morals and ethics is always the safest bet.

Through research, one can easily identify the extent to which leading PR practitioners are held to high moral ground. The codes of conduct for these well-respected organizations are illuminating.

- The Chartered Institute of Public Relations (UK): http://bit.ly/CIPRcc1
- The International Public Relations Association (UK): http://bit.ly/IPRAcc
- The Public Relations Consultants Association: http://bit.ly/PRCAccc
- The Public Relations Society of America: http://bit.ly/PRSA_e1

Ethics in Your Practice and Mine

At least from my point of view, the truth is this: Even if you have sworn to any of these oaths of conduct, there is really nothing to stop you from violating their tenets. That is, unless you are intending to continue to live in the world where ethics and morals are expected, which allows people to trust and rely upon you to provide value to them and "do no harm." Doing harm is obviously bad, and after going in that direction, regaining trust and convincing people to rely on you will be an uphill battle. Therefore, my advice is for you to join me in aiming high and committing to upholding and enforcing equity and honesty.

From there, in my experience, adopting the Boy Scouts' law should take you far, personally and professionally: "A Scout is Trustworthy, Loyal, Helpful, Friendly, Courteous, Kind, Obedient, Cheerful, Thrifty, Brave, Clean, and Reverent."

Exploration

1. Can you think of a time when you heard about someone who had "a reputation"? If so, list a few attributes the person supposedly had, and imagine the impact on the subjects.

2. Name three men and three women who have positive reputations and list the main attribute you think of for each of them.
3. Name five companies you would like to work with that have positive reputations.
4. If you were hired to handle PR or social media for a company known for condoning sexist behavior, what would you do first?
5. Identify five things that can be attributed to a positive business reputation.
6. Can you think of anything negative that might come from a business having a positive reputation?
7. Given two assignments that demand immediate attention where both involve posting a public message on the company's social media accounts, how would you prioritize?
8. Asked by an executive to impact her company's bottom line by consulting on communications, how would you establish the working relationship?
9. Can you think of a company with a positive reputation that failed? Why did it die?
10. Can you think of a company with a negative reputation that prospered? Why did it survive?

Notes

1 Van den Bogaerd, M., & Aerts, W. (2015). Does media reputation affect properties of accounts payable? *European Management Journal*, 33(1), 19–29. https://doi.org/10.1016/j.emj.2014.05.002.
2 The Harris Poll. (2017, February 9). Corporate Reputation Politically Polarized as Companies Wrestle with Taking a Stand for Their Values. *PR Newswire*. https://prn.to/2BdIq6b.
3 McKinney, M. (2017, November 9). Communication Quotes | LeadingThoughts - LeadershipNow.com. *LeadingThoughts - LeadershipNow.Com*. http://bit.ly/leadword.
4 Stewart, P. (n.d.). Potter Stewart Quotes. *BrainyQuote*. Retrieved October 31, 2016, from https://www.brainyquote.com/quotes/potter_stewart_390058.
5 What are the Scout Oath and Scout Law? (2019, December 16). Boy Scouts of America. https://www.scouting.org/about/faq/question10/.
6 Wikipedia contributors. (n.d.). Hippocratic Oath. *Wikipedia*. Retrieved February 26, 2021, from https://en.wikipedia.org/wiki/Hippocratic_Oath.
7 Thunderbird Oath of Honor. (2018, June 1). Thunderbird School of Global Management. http://bit.ly/TB_oath.

2
Creativity

When I think about what is most integral to understanding the work of a communications consultant, the subject of Creativity leaps to the forefront. Of course, virtually all my agency clients have done business in what is widely known as the *creative industry*, so this emphasis has much to do with my experience and interests. Still, there is also a lot of evidence connecting Creativity with business success.[1] To me, it is clearly at the heart of successful strategic communication.

In the service of entertainment companies, design firms, musical, audio, or visual specialists, companies that produce products that have been physical and digital, and others that have brought value to life for customer groups large and small, I have been privileged to work in the exciting place where strategic decision-makers author sales and service-oriented dialogues, either for their own businesses or for others'. Typically, these endeavors start with evaluating core brand identities, and in some cases, they rise to the most sophisticated levels of marketing, including multimillion dollar integrated advertising campaigns and Super Bowl spots. The proliferation of these types of businesses easily substantiates the overall importance of Creativity. Within their operations, Creativity is almost a religion. As a result, to be of service as a communications consultant for them – and any other type of business I can think of – we must understand certain things about Creativity, gain some insights into its nuances, and learn how to apply it in our work.

Creativity in the Creative Industry

By the age of five, the luckiest human beings are aware of what it means to create something. Usually, early into our education, we are nurtured in artistic settings and invited to be creative. How the time flies in those hours when we are given some basic building materials and invited to put our

DOI: 10.4324/9781003177951-2

imaginations to work without limitation; when there are no wrong answers, and what seems most prized is originality… as well as the productive passing of time in an enjoyable way. On the other hand, how unfortunate is it that so much of what is usually called "work" inspires dread? The idea of completing mundane tasks repeatedly, from one day to the next, for pay, is the workday cliché so many people still face. On the bright side, right now, demand for skilled labor (work that requires special training, generally defined as being education beyond high school) is widely on the rise.[2] In that light, education is the key to maximizing satisfaction and wages when it comes to our occupations. If we can learn to be creative and use Creativity at work, that work can become enjoyable.

Serving companies in the creative industry, I have learned that most of their employees are people who see themselves as artists in some way. They may have originally envisioned being professional graphic designers, photographers, writers, or directors, but as one career opportunity led to the next, some application of their talents arose that they chose to focus on. A great example is my longstanding client Erin Sarofsky, who often tells the story about how, after working for several different companies as a staff art director for many years, she seized the opportunity to go freelance, which would allow her to handle assignments without being an employee. When she then encountered a substantial project assignment, she let her potential new client know she was not working for a production company at that time. The client reportedly suggested she set up her own, and soon, the business called Sarofsky Corp. was established in Chicago. I have worked for many companies over the years that had remarkably similar origins; in fact, you can find them all around the world. And as one creative individual proceeds on this path, the pattern is for them to hire others with complementary talents – for example, producers, illustrators, animators, actors, voiceover artists … even accountants, bookkeepers, lawyers, and communications consultants – to support them and their clients.

Another common aspect of these companies is their dedication to Creativity. Indeed, most often, the path to cash flow begins with a potential client issuing a creative briefing, where it is their job (almost always uncompensated) to demonstrate how they would go about fulfilling it (referred to as *pitching*). In this world, usually several creative entities are invited to bid on any given assignment; so, these types of businesses must build their economic model around pitching and bidding, knowing they will only get paid if their pitches win. To a large extent, successful bids rely upon Creativity (among many other key factors we will address, like sound management and operational expertise). For the record, you do not need to do much research to understand how bidding is a key facet of business development for every type of industry under the sun. The difference in bids that win often favors the application of Creativity.

In the creative industry, companies live or die according to their ability to be creative on demand. Near the top of their corporate food chain is at least one creative director who must be capable of going toe-to-toe, intellectually, with the creatives on the client side. Worth noting, business executives are notorious for ranking themselves as superior sources of Creativity over external creative directors. The phenomenon of entrepreneurs proclaiming omniscience is legendary. Still, for various reasons, even the best executives will outsource Creativity, which often takes the form of a creative challenge. To be successful in exploiting such opportunities, creative companies and their employees must remain committed to exploration, investigation, experimentation, invigoration, innovation, learning, and reinvention. In all these pursuits, Creativity is essential.

For all businesses – including communications consulting – most opportunities yield from the interconnected sciences of sales and marketing; here again, Creativity is the pathway to success. If you are going to be put in the position to impact a business using this training, it will come from an enterprising business executive who understands the need to be creative in engaging with certain people. There are bound to be specifics, of course, but embracing the need to be inventive in your work is the prerequisite.

Creativity as Business Practice

The famed American art director, designer, and author George Lois expressed his faith in Creativity's ability to conquer most problems. Through personal experience, I have seen that Creativity is a science: Using standard exercises in its application, the powerful results can bolster a company's success, unleash opportunities, and otherwise convert woes into wins. To better understand Creativity's practice and nuances, let us delve deeper into its use in the creative industry, and in the work of communications consultants.

Whenever I think of this subject, the great John Cleese always comes to mind. This stems from wide exposure to Monty Python and everything viewers experienced as he and his troupe constantly covered new ground with their ideas and performances. There is also a famous speech he has given at different times over the years, which has been widely published.[3] The takeaways are educational, instructive, and engaging, exuding Mr. Cleese's signature intelligence, cultural insights, and comedic genius. In those talks, he illuminated five steps we all can use to make our lives more creative. To summarize:

1. Seek out your own creative place where you can think freely;
2. stay there for an allotted time;
3. acclimate yourself to focusing purely on crafting original work;
4. give yourself positive encouragement for your efforts;
5. and consider the strategic use of humor, with its power to engage audiences instantly.

Back when Simon Needham was still involved as co-founder and executive creative director for the global agency known as ATTIK, he responded to a request from the editors of *Creativity* magazine asking him to define the subject. "To me, Creativity begins with going in a direction that is altogether unique and unexplored," he explained. "It means breaking the rules. A creative person does things in original ways. As it relates to advertising, Creativity is genuinely being able to differentiate yourself from others. Genuine Creativity is behind the things we remember; if it's really creative, people are going to remember it, and they're going to go around telling other people about it."

In *The Idea Book*, author Fredrik Hárén eloquently writes about the world's first Creativity test, citing a speech made over 60 years ago by J.P. Guilford and describing the man as the father of modern Creativity.[4] What was his test? To assess the thinking skills of Air Force pilots with the goal of determining their fitness for certain missions, Mr. Guilford asked them to list as many uses as possible for a brick. For Mr. Lois, Mr. Cleese, Mr. Needham, and anyone else who has worked in the creative industry, such an exercise would present a familiar scenario, where the results of their efforts would aim to surprise and delight anyone who saw them.

Those who embrace such challenges and bring enthusiasm to solving them will excel when it comes to successfully handling strategic communications.

Exploration

1. Name at least three companies you would not consider to be in the creative industry, that have made a positive impression on you by being creative.
2. Name a TV commercial that you recall from the past year or two for its Creativity – or one that disappointed you. How might that commercial's Creativity impact the brand's sales?

3. If you were free to have any creative job – or operate or work for a creative company – what would you choose to do?
4. Imagine you own a farm where you raise lettuce, and name three creative ideas you could use to make people want to buy your produce.
5. Imagine you oversee hiring for a local taco stand, and name three creative ideas you could use to attract great employees.
6. Name at least two sketches or situations you recall from a sitcom or comedy series. Do you feel that humor opened up an interesting subject? If so, what was the subject and how was it opened up?
7. Why do you feel the right "space" is important for being creative – and if you imagine the worst space to be creative in, what could you do to make it more conducive to creativity?
8. Effective problem-solving relies upon being fully present in the moment. Name five ways improving focus and eliminating distractions can impact creative ideas and outcomes.
9. Your situation in life provides some freedoms that others might only dream about. List at least three activities or situations you would miss if you did not have those freedoms.
10. Give yourself five minutes to make a list of uses for a common brick. Go!

Notes

1 Fallon, N. (2016, March 16). How Crucial Is Creativity to Your Business Success? *Business News Daily*. https://shar.es/a1jMfD.
2 Fastest Growing Occupations: Occupational Outlook Handbook. (2020, September 1). U.S. Bureau of Labor Statistics. https://www.bls.gov/ooh/fastest-growing.htm.
3 Video Arts. (2017, June 21). John Cleese on Creativity in Management [Video]. *YouTube*. https://youtu.be/Pb5oIIPO62g.
4 Härén, F. (2006). *The Idea Book* (1st ed.). Interesting.org.

3
Strategy

Something led you to pick up this book, which is focused on sharpening your communications skills and preparing you to use them to make an impact, make good money, and work independently, if you so choose. At the most basic level, achievement usually requires some type of strategy, methodology, or plan of attack … even if it is just deciding to get out of bed or to use your phone to learn something. As we take aim on becoming more successful communicators and consultants, we need to have a firm understanding of the essential role of strategy in shaping our behavior, guiding our decision-making and steering our actions in favorable directions.

By the time I arrived at Homestead Air Force Base as a 19-year-old Reservist, I had graduated from high school, plus Air Force Basic Training and Tech School. No one makes it through high school without knowing how all-encompassing that phase of life is, where a fascinating irony plays out: On one hand, almost everyone fits some model type that seems predestined for a certain fate … while on the other hand, it is fully understood that we are works in progress and our adult lives are blank slates. Personally, I had a goal of going on to college, and I knew that getting there was almost entirely up to me. As the scenarios played out and I failed to win a scholarship, joining the Air Force Reserves and taking advantage of the G.I. Bill provided a means to pay for school. It was a simple strategy, and thankfully, it worked.

My first job in the Air Force was in fuels, which fell under the service's Tactical Air Command department. Eventually it sunk in that refueling our squadron of fighter aircraft fit within the military's arsenal of tactics, while some of the more intellectual aspects of planning and operations were conducted through the Strategic Air Command. As a working member of a large force, this separation of functions helped me begin to understand organizational leadership. Some years later, the vital importance of strategy leapt to the forefront of all my business endeavors.

DOI: 10.4324/9781003177951-3

Communications Strategy in Education

A standard requirement for anyone who attends college is making the tremendously impactful decision to choose exactly what they intend to study. Faced with this or that degree prospect and the completion of specific coursework to attain it, many procrastinate by remaining "undeclared." Necessarily, over time, pressure mounts to pick a major. From the very beginning, I was certain that the communications field was my domain, and after reading through the catalog time and time again, I chose a major of Radio/Television, while also deciding to minor in Journalism (at The University of Central Florida or UCF, Journalism was covered under Public Relations).

Working to pay the bills while attending classes at night, and doing Air Force Reserve drills one weekend per month, those combined experiences helped me gain an insight: Working in a TV or Radio station was not what I had in mind. Somewhere after getting my associates degree and reading my catalog more thoroughly, an epiphany led me to change my major to Film. At the time, I was holding down a full-time job … and according to UCF Film professor Mike Sullivan, that was not going to cut it for a Film major. Heeding his advice, I undertook a very rocky career transition into the freelance world. It took me three more years to graduate (six total for a four-year degree), but when I hit the finish line, I had earned two B.A. degrees. More importantly, I had successfully employed my primary strategy, which was seizing every opportunity to achieve my goal of positioning myself for success in the film, television, and communications industries. That dogged approach of wringing every possible benefit from my hard-earned higher education is a lesson I want to emphasize. Here is what I encourage:

- Determine what you want to do and who you want to be and make it your mission to constantly move yourself that direction.

These days, the opportunities to learn new things and transform ourselves are vast and limitless. There may be legitimate impediments preventing you from moving forward; my advice is to steel your strength and address them with every fiber of your being, until you are in position to learn. From there, soak up everything you can and use it all to the best or your ability.

Communications Strategy in Career Planning

To continue illuminating these ideas and hopefully inspiring your next-level career development, let us briefly revisit a couple more of my career hurdles.

After my wife and I relocated to Los Angeles, I came to two different places where my strategies varied based on circumstances. Looking back, I can see that as I arrived at each new crossroads, I was altering my core identity.

Having earned some respectable positions among the crews behind 40 hours' worth of episodic television production in Orlando, Beth and I shipped out to Hollywood, lock, stock, and barrel. My dream at that time was to be a screenwriter, and I had some original screenplays and one spec TV teleplay under my belt, along with quite a bit of experience writing nonfiction articles that had earned some money … and writing and submitting creative writing, that had only earned experience. Although I had made friends with many major talents in "the industry," five months into the LA move, I was completely unhinged. Pedaling my scripts and networking led me nowhere viable, and my only hope was landing a job. Miraculously, I was hired to handle PR and marketing for a family-owned film lab in Hollywood. To earn that job, I had to convince the owners that it was my dream to attain it. There is no doubt I was attempting to "stop the bleeding" in my failed attempt to seize my true aspirations as a screenwriter, but obviously, if I wanted that job, I had to present myself as the ideal candidate. That is exactly what I did, over some very tough competition.

Here is my takeaway from this bout: If you want a job, you must absolutely focus on making and presenting yourself as the ideal candidate … because you can guarantee that is what your competitors will do.

I had learned to maximize learning experiences and to "Aim High" in all career endeavors, so over the next two years, I nabbed exciting positions at two more companies … first as a marketing director for a creative production company working in television, then as an account executive for high-tech PR firm The Terpin Group (TTG). In the years since 1999, I have communicated my gratefulness to Michael Terpin many times while also acknowledging the vital experience and insights I gained working at his firm. It was his General Manager Mike Garfinkel who hired me. Together with Office Manager Lori-Ann Harbridge and the other accomplished professionals on their staff, they all taught me the ropes of landing and managing PR accounts.

Next came another crossroads, where I felt ready to return to self-employment. Obviously, whenever I have sought to engage clients as a professional consultant dedicated to public and media relations, I have never started by telling them about *my screenplays*. Landing clients has required me to convincingly demonstrate that I was the best person to help them tell their mission-essential stories and present viable means for getting them out into the world, primarily through shrewd promotional marketing and earned media coverage. So, my strategy with the launch of The Darnell Works Agency was to position myself as a spectacular communications consultant capable of generating monumental results, and then to validate my skills and qualifications every day.

Thanks to my efforts while at TTG, and the graciousness of Mr. Terpin and Mr. Garfinkel supporting my departure, I had my first client the day I left their employment. Over the year that followed, I had a lot of opportunities to advance my reputation – much of that having to do with being in Los Angeles, and having a powerful, industry gate-crashing fire starter in San Francisco by the name Lisa Cleff as dear friend and stalwart advocate. With business on the rise, life also got much more interesting; Beth and I learned we were expecting, and decided to move to North Carolina, where our little one could grow up with cousins and more family nearby.

At this juncture, I devised a new strategy for my business that has served me well ever since. Essentially, I committed to being extraordinary in my job for each of my roster clients, and to keeping my roster small, to allow me to fulfill that. This mindset is also a talking point I raise with clients and anyone who asks about my business. Many companies aim to grow and add staff – I know from personal and shared experiences that it is one thing to manage a staff, and another to manage accounts. Of course, there is also the business to run, and in my case, I have my life and business partner Beth to help with that.

When it comes to exploring the crossroads you face and finding the best strategy and tactics to serve your interests, that is something else I am keen to help with. In light of my story, consider this widely held idea: True success means *enjoying* one's vocation. Through these endeavors, aiming to serve my needs and interests, I have found a job I enjoy thoroughly, where I am extremely well rewarded. That is prosperity I am thankful for every day.

Communications Strategy in Business

Working at TTG, not only did I hone each of the steps necessary to consistently place stories in targeted, high-profile media outlets (those steps being strategic planning, research, building relationships with journalists and influencers, pitching, promoting, and client relations), I also came to see how the PR function fit among the other aspects of marketing. The great book *Advertising and Promotion: An Integrated Marketing Communications Perspective*, from George and Michael Belch, goes very deep in illuminating every nuance of marketing communications and educating readers on how all the facets work together. Since PR fits within marketing, and you are sure to be weighing in on marketing on behalf of any client you serve, you will want to familiarize yourself with all details presented in the Belchs' book. We will drill deeper in the chapter on Integrated Marketing (10).

Here, I want to share some insights that came to me from Mirren Business Development, a consultancy in New York specializing in providing sales training and resources for agencies. For many years, Mirren has used its annual business conference to conduct research into ad agencies' biggest challenges. As part of this discussion, consider the example of the award-winning television series, *Mad Men*. The dialogues and maneuverings between agencies and their clients presented there reflect America's creative industry in the 1960s, when the powers of media and communications were already well established. The propaganda of World War II provides yet another fascinating lens into the sublime virtues of messaging, especially when combined with media. In his groundbreaking book, *The Medium is the Massage*, Marshall McLuhan wrote: "Media, by altering the environment, evoke in us unique ratios of sense perceptions. The extension of any one sense alters the way we think and act – the way we perceive the world. When these ratios change, men change."[1]

Watching *Mad Men*, audiences quickly realize that over the past six decades, the world has changed radically. Overt male dominance, rampant use of cigarettes and alcohol in the workplace aside, those episodes also showcase a world of strategic problem-solving that is devoid of personal computers and cell phones. Today, we must constantly commit to dealing with the ins and outs of digitalization and mobility. With all the phenomenal alterations of media, men and women, marketing has changed, and so have agencies.

On the day in 2009 when I received an email from Mirren's Managing Partner Brent Hodgins revealing insights from their latest research, I sensed a paradigm shift. In a nutshell, for agencies seeking to win business, it heavily emphasized the heightened importance of strategy, even above creative ideas.

As I spread Mr. Hodgins' message among peers and clients, the hunch was confirmed. While change has always been part of agency life, at that time, the reliance upon creative development and execution was taking a back seat to strategy. In other words, to really help brands market themselves successfully, the plans to be put into effect to achieve the desired results had become imperative.

From my perspective, all of this validates Mr. McLuhan's premise: Media, the world, and people all are changing, and the means of engaging them for marketing purposes are being forced to evolve.

According to experts in marketing, there is a strategy that can be employed to cut through the confusion prompted by change, and that is to focus on building and maintaining relationships with customers.[2] Let us go a step further in fortifying the role of public relations in helping virtually any business succeed.

Whether we are talking about business brands or personal brands, there is a story to be told. It needs to be one that will engage the target audiences, and ideally, set the subject apart in authentic, sustainable ways that encourage others to engage with them. When applying for a job, when attempting to build a consultancy and attract clients, when helping another person or business go to market, exactly how you pursue the goal is absolutely of the essence. Assuming you agree, we are on the same page, ready to progress.

I previously mentioned Justin Meredith's recommendation for me on LinkedIn. It is relevant here to share the second part of his kind feedback in my regard: "He's an expert at determining the best course of action ultimately leading to successful results." As consultants, we must make a company's communications with others effective and interesting for the customers' purposes – while serving the company's bottom-line objectives strategically.

Exploration

1. How did you get your start in your career?
2. How did you wind up in your current profession?
3. What is your current guiding "life strategy" that is most important to you?
4. Describe one situation when you had to be creative – how did that moment impact your life?
5. What type of business opportunity is most attractive to you, and how do you explain your interest?
6. Name an insight about yourself, a partner or a business entity that has driven you into action.
7. Describe one situation when you faced hardship – what did you learn or do to move forward?
8. What would you say has been your greatest career achievement?
9. Please share a favorite quote or mantra and explain what it means to you.
10. Please share a favorite work of art (can be a book, movie, song, album, painting), and explain what it means to you.

Notes

1 McLuhan, M., Fiore, Q., & Agel, J. (1967). *The Medium Is the Massage: An Inventory of Effects* (1st ed.). Bantam Books.
2 ClickSquared. (2012, December 10). The Changing Nature of Campaign Management. *SlideShare*. http://bit.ly/CNcMgmt.

4
Personal Brands and Branding

Hearing from friends who are unable to find work is always troubling. To help, I have organized lists of articles, videos, and other resources they can use to put themselves on better paths – ones more of their choosing, that will challenge them to learn valuable new skill sets designed to help them stand apart from crowds while also making them more valuable to employers. With time, this approach has come into better focus. Nowadays, in discussions aiming to help others learn how to get their careers on track for the future, I usually begin by talking about personal branding. This organized system of innovating from the ground up is also a highly effective means for discussing what I do for clients as a communications consultant.

While the Public Relations profession has a long history, I have found that a great deal of general uncertainty exists about what it encompasses and how it works. So, in a book aiming to help people succeed today and tomorrow by learning to embrace and employ the principals of successful business communications, delving straight into personal branding will illuminate much of what this job entails, and demonstrate how it all works together. If you can learn to establish, cultivate, and effectively manage your own personal brand, you will have a good handle on the basic skill set required to do these things for a company.

What Is a Brand?

You do know what a brand is, right? Thinking of it first as the unique symbols used to permanently mark livestock as belonging to a certain ranch, a brand often represents a company or some key characteristic that identifies that company in the minds of consumers. For example, for Coca-Cola, the brand is its signature logo, the Coca-Cola bottle, and at least to some people, the idea of happiness. For better or for worse, brands do register emotional responses. The YouGov Brand Index reports on the most beloved brands from one year to the next. In recent times, the top four have consistently included Amazon, Google, Netflix, and YouTube.

As a further step in thinking more about all that is represented by the term brand, the brand strategy and design firm Lippincott encourages its clients to think of a brand as possibility. To learn what they mean, visit this blog post, and look at the company's "What is a brand" video:

- Explore brand as possibility with Lippincott – https://up.darnellworks.com/?p=3872

For the idea of "brand as possibility" to have meaning, a brand must be thoughtfully conceived and professionally managed; it must present itself, its products, and services strategically; and it must consistently perform well and provide value to its customers. Clearly, these discussions can get quite lofty, but one thing is certain: Presenting a company or a person as a well-defined brand is a key to leveraging powerful storytelling and reputation management for maximum benefit. Also, if it all sounds complicated, remember these words attributed to Leonardo da Vinci: "Simplicity is the ultimate sophistication."

As we begin to think about applying the key concepts of brands to ourselves, I invite you to spend some time (I suggest at least an hour) exploring the videos at the top of this article, as well as the stories it references.

- Brand thyself – https://up.darnellworks.com/?p=2293

Bear in mind, there is much more information there than anyone needs to comprehend and begin applying the essential ideas. While it may seem overwhelming, remember that any intelligence you gain on this subject is going to supercharge your knowledge and abilities to elevate yourself and all those you serve.

Heeding the advice presented in those articles and resources, you can grasp all the main ideas of personal branding and be ready to begin putting them to use. Before venturing there, you might like to see a few examples of how everything can add up once you have successfully applied the lessons. For the first of those, I invite you to check out the web presence for New York Times bestselling author and TV producer Lee Goldberg at http://leegoldberg.com. Next, here is my personal website (http://www.rkdarnell.com) along with my business website (https://www.darnellworks.com). Finally, sit back and enjoy a lovely, cinematic series of short films that put John Malkovich on the spot as he takes on the challenges of personal branding, and ultimately succeeds: http://bit.ly/JxHJMss. I will refer to Mr. Malkovich's beautifully illustrated situation and his demonstrated approaches in sections to come.

The Basics of Personal Branding – Step 1: Brand Development

There are many firms like Lippincott, which specialize in providing brand development (think, "research and strategic planning") and branding (think, "action") services for their clients. And while I also mentioned the notion of simplicity earlier, when it comes to the practice of brand development, thoroughness and diligence are essential – especially since these efforts provide the underlying platform for every communication and promotional effort to come. In this chapter, I am aiming to cover this material expediently, and lead you through it matter-of-factly, with the goal of having a personal example to draw from fresh in your mind. In an upcoming chapter 7, I will expand the discussion more formally to illuminate the approaches experts use in exploring brand development and branding for businesses. Because businesses tend to involve a lot more people and factors, those approaches are more expansive; however, all the key steps are the same.

The POSTAR model (Positioning, Objectives, Strategies, Tactics, Administration, Results) provides a framework that allows us to move from research through strategic planning and into action methodically and effectively, and it is a system that has long been used in organizing and assessing campaigns. Another methodology I encountered in the U.S. Air Force which is used to develop training programs is called Instructional Systems Design (ISD). Its framework is similar to POSTAR, using a phased approach that proceeds in this order: Analysis, Design, Development, Implementation, Evaluation (or ADDIE).

Illustration of the ADDIE conceptual framework, courtesy of UK-based learning and organizational development specialist Mike Morrison.[1]

Analysis

Let's begin with step one: Analysis or Positioning in the POSTAR model. Essentially, this is an honest assessment of what you care about, how you want to define yourself, what you want to achieve and who you are wishing to reach through your efforts. In the long-form Squarespace ad featuring

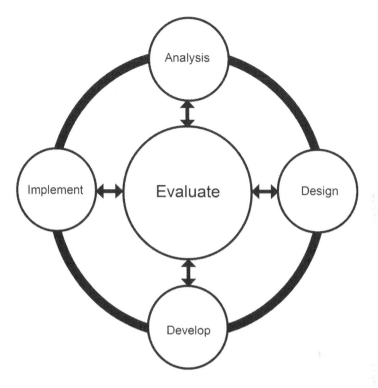

Figure 1 The ADDIE Instructional Design Model. Morrison, M. (2015, September 3). The ADDIE Instructional Design Model #HRBlog. RapidBI. https://rapidbi.com/the-addie-instructional-design-model-hrblog/.

Mr. Malkovich entitled "Make Your Next Move," there is a moment at the :21 mark where the hero pauses for a moment, sitting on his bed and staring into his laptop. From context, we know he is thinking of achieving something, and most people will easily understand that the famous actor known for being a celebrity and having a strong, self-driven personality might find "switching gears" in his career to be a difficult challenge. This makes his scenario very poignant for us all. To successfully discover what defines you, what drives you, and where you want to go, there is no choice but to dive in.

The concept of applying the science of brand development to individuals was brought to my attention by author and speaker Tom Peters, whose 1997 "The Brand Called You" article in Fast Company (included in my "Brand thyself" roundup) rang the bell loudly and clearly.[2] Reading his fervent treatise, I felt the urgent need to spearhead my own marketing campaign. Because the first steps of Analysis can be difficult to address, practitioners have learned to embrace the idea of differentiation. Even at the highest levels, finding what is unique about a brand compared to its competitors is a key in what becomes its simplified brand identity at the core of its communications.

In his book *Frames of Mind: The Theory of Multiple Intelligence*, Howard Gardner defines nine different types of intelligence.[3] Can you think of a distinct type of intelligence that applies to you, and to others you deal with regularly?

Table 1 Personal Brand Analysis

Facets of Brand Discovery	Description	Malkovich Example	You
Current identity	Use words that your biggest "fans" use to define your core strengths and expertise; perhaps include your *intelligence type*, groups you belong to, work experience, honors, hobbies	Actor; serious; accomplished; dramatic; focused; famous; thoughtful	
Desired identity	Who/what do you aspire to be?	Fashion designer	
Unique facets	How are you different? This is imperative.	Middle-aged; celebrity; American; very interested in fashion design; hot-headed; highly successful	
Values offered to your target audience	What values come from knowing or working with you, from the perspective of others?	Serious pro with a recognized name, whose presence and association will command attention; fashion design talent	
Claim your identity	Will you use your name, your philosophy, your expertise, a unique phrase you made up? Remember, it should last a lifetime.	johnmalkovich.com	

To ensure your foundation is as strong as possible, it is highly advised to identify essential traits and insights. The DiSC Profile is a simple exercise anyone can complete to gain insights into their unique behavioral tendencies.[4] Since it evaluates one's acuity around the pillars of Dominance, Influence, Steadiness, and Conscientiousness, knowing your DiSC style can reveal knowledge that is wise to address. I will also point out the obvious here: If you agree that understanding this type of knowledge regarding oneself is intelligent, also bear in mind that the others you work with, and all of those you seek to build connections with, have their own DiSC styles. You can learn more about 12 different DiSC styles here: http://www.bit.ly/DiSC12. My own assessment identified me as a "high C," which is fleshed out in more detail here: http://www.bit.ly/DiSC-C.

So, as you sit down and attempt to distill your essence and your imperatives, it is sure to help as you use differentiation, consider the types of intelligence that best describe you, explore your unique behavioral tendencies, and prioritize your goals and factor in favorite pastimes and associations you belong to. Now, complete the personal branding "Analysis" exercise.

The Basics of Personal Branding – Step 2: Brand Creation

To guide us through these next steps, I will divulge a few personal examples from my own experience. On the day when I left the high-tech PR firm The Terpin Group (TTG) in Los Angeles to launch my own practice, I turned 34 years old. My professional experience included everything I had done for that high profile firm and its clientele, and other work spanning TV entertainment; film, television and live event production and post-production; advertising and promotion; photojournalism; training and public affairs in the Air Force Reserves; and in college, writing a humor column and organizing, running, and promoting a popular cinema society and its events over a couple of years. With so many opportunities to work with professionals and brands in meaningful ways, and having tried a few different times to brand myself, I had a lot of knowledge to draw upon. I planned to continue using "Darnell Works," as I had done in college and while building my freelance career in Florida. I added "Agency," and created a simple logo using the DWA initials. Knowing the value of spectacular imagery, I decided to see what I could find from NASA, based on an understanding that much of its beautiful photography of space is in the public domain. My first business card in the new professional iteration used an astronaut floating in Earth orbit, and referred to some of the main tenets of Instructional Systems Design I had learned about in the Air Force: Objectives, Strategies and Results. I also added a distinguishing tag line which I felt offered a unique differentiation: Dynamic Public Relations. While TTG was dynamic – I knew I offered extra agility, dynamism, and flexibility in accommodating budgets.

The offer presented on my business card worked, and even at a massive conference for marketers and designers who focus on the TV entertainment industry, I had people looking at that astronaut, reading those words, and saying "yes, let's talk." From there, I was invited to bid on some accounts, and

Table 2 The Copy Platform

Section	Description	Your Version for Personal Brand
Client	Who is this for?	(You!)
Objectives:	What are you aiming to accomplish with the story/project?	
Target audience:	Who is the story/project intended to reach and engage?	
Sales theme:	Often, the headline – package the story/project around its main news value	
Bonus items:	Is there something else that's relevant to the story and makes it more interesting?	
Positioning:	How is this story/project and/or its subject unique compared to other similar stories/projects and subjects?	
Approach:	What form will the story/project take? A business card? A website? An ad campaign?	

The Copy Platform addresses all branding and campaign development elements in your writing.

with the contract experience acquired at TTG and some polishing approved by my lawyer, I was able to start expanding my roster almost immediately.

Soon, as I continued working with more designer types, I received an in-depth critique of my brand. According to one, my font choices did not match. That short point begins to address the expansive realm of graphic design, and while the encounter was maddening for me, it led to me doing more homework and eventually making some changes in the spirit of having more attractive materials.

Ready or not, it is time to take a pass at applying the Creative Process toward bringing your personal brand identity to life. This process encapsulates the approach where we identify the problem, conduct our research, and then present a solution. Often in the creative industry, one will see this represented as a cycle, indicating that the process is intended to repeat endlessly.

I picked up another amazing tool in college that has been priceless in helping me formulate virtually every client-driven story I have ever written. Referred to as the Copy Platform, you can see it on the previous page.[5]

Design (Objectives, Strategies)

In the Copy Platform, you are asked to state your objectives, specifying exactly what you are setting out to accomplish with your actions. While I did mention the idea that the people you work with and those you want to engage have their own DiSC styles, we have not gone very far in addressing target audiences. What you are aiming to achieve is going to require that someone hire you or buy your products, right? In this field of communications consulting, success relies on engaging and landing customers. For more on the importance of focusing on the right audiences, I encourage you to spend some time with this article and the video presented by author, entrepreneur, and teacher Seth Godin.

- Sharing secrets: Know your audience! – https://up.darnellworks.com/?p=3967

To seasoned marketers, engaging in strategic communications without considering the target audience is like driving with closed eyes. Indeed, there is a large and mission-critical aspect of the marketing industry that focuses on qualitative (exploring roots and causes) and quantitative (measuring and presenting data) research. To progress with brand development effectively, we must assess those we intend to engage, learn what they care about, and position ourselves to provide value to them. A smart approach to this aim is creating customer profiles, where some diligence goes into fleshing out a vision of exactly who you are trying to reach.

- How to Create Customer Profiles to Reach Your Target Audience – http://bit.ly/CustPf[6]

Knowing what you want to achieve and who you are intending to target, let's revisit our earlier discussion about strategy. My own strategy upon leaving TTG was to pursue clients in the creative industry as a PR consultant and establish new working relationships according to specific terms. Key components of my branding efforts were a name; contact information; a photo of me; a bio; a logo; a website featuring all the above and portfolio materials; a profile on LinkedIn; a business card; and additional promotional materials. To be effective, it was essential that each of those pieces was authentic and unique, while also being consistent in virtually every way, including theme, message, tone, and fonts.

Let's also draw on what we have learned about creativity and move ahead in solving the problems necessary to render these elements for your use in strategically pursuing your objectives.

Develop Your Key Components

First, remember that one of the main reasons to develop your personal brand is to readily communicate whatever is most unique about you, and as much as possible, to present those distinct qualities by conveying what they mean to others, with the goal of creating viable connections. When I was blazing my new trail with DWA, I communicated my Instructional Systems Design and PR backgrounds through words: Objectives, Strategies, Results, The Darnell Works Agency, Dynamic Public Relations. The astronaut in Earth orbit reflected my values of aiming high, being highly trained, skilled, qualified, and specialized. It is almost like that astronaut was me ... but instead of the logo being for NASA, it was for the company I invented.

Perhaps like Mr. Malkovich or Oprah, you will just focus your personal brand identity on your name ... or maybe you will follow the lead of Stacy Ann Ferguson (Fergie) or Aubrey Drake Graham (Drake).

Another mission-critical component is your email address. While I tend to think of this as something everyone knows about, experience compels me to remind you: Choose wisely. There are simple solutions (gmail, aol, icloud) and more advanced ones (involving your own domain, like the one set up by my wife's cousin Paul at Kiefert.com). Along with being perfectly acceptable, Gmail is widely used. Whatever you choose, the key is to find a relatively short version or abbreviation of your name, or at the very least, something that does not sound unprofessional. One example that makes me laugh is my cousin Joel Ridings' address: ToadsMounts@hotmail.com. His nickname is Toad, and he does taxidermy. Even knowing these things, the first time I saw that email handle, I blushed. The point is, before locking in something that you intend to use professionally, it is a good idea to invite several others to share their first impressions.

Phone numbers also carry a surprising amount of weight and meaning in the business world. Ideally, you want to have a dedicated line where you know that if you get a call, you need to handle it professionally. I'm sure you can imagine my surprise many years ago when I called a supposedly prestigious photographer and encountered this voicemail greeting: "Who the hell is this, and what the hell do you want? Leave a message." My translation was: This rude person has no interest in building meaningful relationships or doing business. Take a lesson from that guy, and put a telephone answering system in place that is thoughtful and allows people to provide a message in the event they miss you. Avoid having anyone encounter the unprofessional situation where your mailbox is full, or not set up. Also, if you are available to field the call, answer it – and be ready to meet a new best friend. Chinese philosopher Lao Tzu said that the journey of a thousand miles begins with a single step; I can honestly report that almost every one of my client relationships for the past 20+ years has started either with an email message or a phone call.

The rise of social media has led to mainstream awareness of the phenomenon of people taking pictures of ourselves. Why do we do this, and why has it become such a big deal? First, every social media account we set out to use wants us to have a profile picture, and we now all have these phones that are so handy for snapping them. While picture-taking and sharing is multiplying thanks to technology and the human desire to connect, the world has long been obsessed with visuals ... especially faces. As you assemble your core set of essentials, do yourself a tremendous favor by creating a photo that is sharp, clear, high quality, professional-looking and – if possible – stylized to match your values. The technology we all have ready access to also makes it extremely easy to produce video, and there is unlimited evidence on YouTube of enterprising communicators like Sunny Lenarduzzi (https://sunny-lenarduzzi.com) creating exemplary presentations that have set the subjects apart – and in many cases, launched their careers. Communicating in front of a camera is not necessarily for everyone ... which is a great reason for you to make every reasonable effort to use that medium to distinguish yourself.

Next comes your bio – a short write-up that encapsulates your history while also underscoring your professional qualifications. For anyone you meet, it is the polished version of what you would say when asked, "What's your story?" Having prepared this, you will be ready to seize face-to-face and online opportunities to present yourself meaningfully. I am a fan of the bio presented at https://johnmalkovich.com/about – it accomplishes a lot, very concisely and eloquently, which is what you would expect for this well-known icon. Even for his biggest fans, there are surprises in store. Bear in mind, there are resumes and curriculum vitae (CVs), which are usually even longer and more detailed; bios tend to be much shorter. To help my clients create theirs, I have developed this set of questions.

1. Where are you from, what are the main facets of your education, including graduation years?
2. What is your work history – list companies, year started and left, and positions held.
3. Major (and/or particularly cool/fun) credits/feats/accomplishments/developments at each company you have worked for?
4. If not already covered, awards and other interesting career achievements?
5. Please provide details of association memberships or serious hobbies with years, roles, highlights?
6. Most recent project(s) you have worked on, whether for work or of a personal nature?
7. Any other major interests that help define you? If so, list each one and its importance.

In my experience, many bios start at the beginning of a person's life and work to the present, but another approach is to begin with the present and work backward to the roots. Based on your answers to the questions above, choose one of these approaches and take a shot at creating your professional life summary. Rest assured, none of this effort will go to waste; this content will be used widely, to your benefit.

When it comes to creating a logo, let Nick Carson, former editor of *Computer Arts* magazine and chair of judges for the Brand Impact Awards, be your guide on a survey of expert logo design tips.

- Logo design: All you need to know – https://bit.ly/MakeLog1

There are plenty of inexpensive software packages available to help you design a logo, and naturally, many websites as well that will immediately start generating unique ideas. Here are a few of them:

- https://www.top10bestlogodesign.com
- https://www.tailorbrands.com
- https://looka.com/logo-maker
- https://www.logaster.com/logo

A good logo helps to present the essence of a brand in a unique way, using things like fonts, letters, numbers, shapes, symbols, forms, and colors – alone or in odd combinations – to communicate something special about the entity, simply and elegantly. As Mr. Carson points out, while the logo is just the beginning of a branding identity, it is also the entry point into the brand's world ... and a smart visual summation of everything it represents.

There is a great book filled with inspiration from advertising pioneer Paul Arden named *It's Not How Good You Are, It's How Good You Want to Be*. Paraphrasing its author, staying true to a subject is essential, and that is also the means for creating something that will remain relevant over time.[7]

All in all, I encourage you to fully embrace this and other challenges we will address together, knowing they can produce results that will raise your career to unforeseen heights.

Now, recall your state of mind from the assignment to devise ideas for creatively repurposing a brick. Think of your best idea and your worst. Consider exactly how you wish to be perceived and let your imagination flow. Still blocked? Reference some of the giants mentioned in this book for brainstorming ideas, like these: play with humor; instead of solving the problem, make it worse; look around and use what you see in your creative solution.

Here is one more idea that may be fruitful: Visit https://www.behance.net, the online platform where artists showcase their work. For every project shown on the landing page, there is an artist listed, and by clicking that artist's name, you will see how they represent themselves. Sometimes it is a personal photo, or if they are a photographer or illustrator, one of their best pieces. From all these sources, find an approach that you feel represents you. For my personal brand, like Mr. Malkovich, I have used my handwriting and signature.

Now it is time to create your personal roost on the Internet. This domain of yours need not cost money nor a great deal of time, but it is a vital aspect of connecting with others, as it allows them to find all the other gemstones you have been collecting and polishing through this exercise. Here are a few places you can register your spot, which it is then your assignment to customize according to everything you have developed to represent your personal brand.

- https://about.me – free, simple, single page customizable landing page
- https://www.behance.net – free, portfolio site in wide use in global design industry
- https://wordpress.com – free, powerful, upgradeable site for blogging and more
- http://www.wix.com – free, powerful, upgradeable site for blogging and more
- https://www.weebly.com – free, powerful, upgradeable site for blogging and more
- https://tumblr.com – free, powerful, upgradeable site for blogging and more

If you go with a free listing on either of the first three choices above, you may wind up with something like https://about.me/rkdarnell, https://www.behance.net/dwagency, or https://rkdarnell.wordpress.com. There is no cost involved in setting up or maintaining any of those outposts, and to me, they are solid approaches for the branding objectives of individuals or even small businesses. Bear in mind, you may want to take the step of purchasing your own domain, so that yourname.com can be used to direct visitors where you want them to go (I can point rkdarnell.com and darnellworks.com to any of the sites above), and you can also set up you@yourname.com for your email. To explore purchasing your domain name, setting up forwarding and email services, I recommend https://www.networksolutions.com.

The business- and employment-oriented social network LinkedIn has grown in prominence to the point of being an essential career-building asset for yours truly, even though I have never spent a dime on it. I use the site daily in essential ways: When I meet someone new through project development or networking, I find them on the site and send them an invitation to connect … and I also get to see their career background and so much more, including learning if we have contacts in common. Beyond having my own career background, up-to-date bio, and photograph on my listing, I also make efforts to post updates weekly … and to acknowledge updates my contacts are sharing through comments or "likes." If you are unfamiliar with LinkedIn, it is time to change that. Begin by thinking of it as an online home for your resume and spend some time to add a profile that reflects everything from your resume that is worth sharing. Connect there with friends, coworkers, former employers and even people you meet in everyday life where you may have common professional interests. Want to make yourself look even more polished? You can customize the direct link leading to your LinkedIn profile by following the directions here: https://bit.ly/LI-4u. Then, take your presence to the next level by providing Recommendations for others you know and respect, and asking your key contacts to do the same for you: https://bit.ly/LI-REC.

It is probably a safe bet to assume that more than 95% of the world's business cards have been produced without the subject doing half of the homework we have undertaken. Remember, this exercise is meant to produce a profile for you that is useful, while also giving you a better understanding of the communications consultant job. If you anticipate starting and operating a consulting business, you probably do not need a business card or promotional materials like postcards or flyers for your personal brand; that is, unless you will be attempting to develop business opportunities that relate more to what you do personally (creating your own fashion line, for one example). Assuming you can imagine good uses for communications tools branded with your personal identity, start here.

- https://spark.adobe.com/make/card-maker/business/
- https://www.vistaprint.com
- https://www.youprint.com
- https://www.moo.com

Implement (Tactics, Administration) and Evaluate (Results)

If you have actively participated in all the prescribed diligence and tasks, you now have a lot to show for your efforts. Knowing what your objectives are and who you wish to engage with, you now have information and materials you have developed strategically and creatively, and you are ready to put them to use. This is where the practices of integrated marketing come into play. Remembering the idea of simplicity being the ultimate sophistication, think of the easiest ways you can achieve your objectives, and use the key components of your personal brand to address them.

Both the ADDIE and POSTAR development frameworks emphasize the necessity of measuring results, evaluating effectiveness of the overall plans, and refinement aimed at delivering the most effective results possible. Since marketing is a continuous cycle involving ongoing innovation, measurement and refinement, the discussions we have had about the importance of reputation management, ethics, creativity, and strategy are designed to serve as a solid foundation. When we approach communications from the perspective of doing what is right, being endlessly creative and strategic, the diligent application of brand development science leads us to creating information, materials, and content that can be used to develop meaningful relationships with clients, customers, and new friends.

Our journey can now progress to the ideas of applying these sound communications principals to our work for others, whether as a communications consultant or in your own unique ways, complementing your passions and interests.

Exploration

1. Think about the brands identified as being among the most beloved ones – Amazon, Google, Netflix, YouTube. What is the best thing a brand can do for people?
2. Why do you feel that evaluation is such an important part of brand development?
3. Finding out what is most unique about a person or a brand is a vital key in developing an identity and even a marketing plan. What is most unique about Amazon, Google, Netflix, and YouTube, respectively?
4. Before designing a campaign, why is it important to understand the target audience?
5. What strategy do you have in mind to pursue and use to achieve your objectives?
6. When it comes to solving problems, explain which is more important – analysis or creativity.
7. Shaping perceptions in others' minds is both an art and a science. List ten alternative job titles for a restroom attendant – and take this lesson to heart in your work for yourself and others.
8. Think of any website you have seen for a person and name three things you like most about it.
9. If you have not already done this, go on LinkedIn and write a recommendation for someone (tips here: https://bit.ly/RecRock).
10. For the website listed in your answer to question eight, provide three ideas of things the proprietor might change to build better, more meaningful connections to readers.

Notes

1 Morrison, M. (2015, September 3). The ADDIE Instructional Design Model #HR-Blog. *RapidBI*. https://rapidbi.com/the-addie-instructional-design-model-hrblog/.

2 Peters, T. (1997, August 8). The Brand Called You. *Fast Company*. https://www.fastcompany.com/28905/brand-called-you.
3 Gardner, H.E. (2011). *Frames of Mind: The Theory of Multiple Intelligences* (3rd ed.). Basic Books.
4 What is the DiSC assessment? (n.d.). Discprofile.Com. Retrieved February 26, 2021, from https://www.discprofile.com/what-is-disc.
5 Meeske, M.D., & Norris, R.C. (1987). *Copywriting for the Electronic Media: A Practical Guide* (Wadsworth Series in Mass Communication). Wadsworth Pub. Co.
6 Ciotti, G. (2019, January 6). How to Create Customer Profiles to Reach Your Target Audience. *Convince & Convert*. http://bit.ly/CustPf.
7 Arden, P. (2003). *It's Not How Good You Are, It's How Good You Want to Be* (1st ed.). Phaidon Press.

Part 2

The Arena

Topics Covered

Leadership and Management 49
Objectives 59
Business Brands and Branding 67
Business Development 80
Customer Service 89
Integrated Marketing in Action 97
Cash Flow and Project Flow 107

5
Leadership and Management

Welcome to the larger world of business and commerce – where the efforts of a communications consultant hit the street and/or the metaverse, and rise, fall, or go unnoticed, as the case may be. In this section, we will probe the core aspects of business operations by showcasing some of the best applications from my research and professional experiences, in the hope of helping you better understand what to look for among potential employers and clients.

In the simplest form, leadership is about guiding, and management is about directing skillfully. Applying those ideas to modern history and searching for luminary leaders, individuals like Jeff Bezos, Richard Branson, Bill and Melinda Gates, Steve Jobs, Elon Musk, Barack and Michelle Obama, and Oprah Winfrey spring to mind. Certainly, each of these people has his or her own way of leading and managing, and their stories have taken on legendary proportions.

While I will not attempt to distill the unique leadership secrets of these illustrious achievers, I will illuminate some ideas about leadership frameworks I view as uniquely successful. From there, we will explore a few episodes demonstrating the adoption of those frameworks – and some others where things could have turned out a lot better for everyone involved, if they had been put into effect.

Sign 1 of Successful Leadership: A Clear, Practical, and Integral Mission

As we have discussed, renown can have far-reaching impact on a company's fate. Among the attributes of a positive reputation is a sense of the entity having excellent leadership, a clear vision for the future, and favorable

DOI: 10.4324/9781003177951-5

market opportunities. As such, companies that build positive perceptions among their external audiences are great sources for valuable leadership insights.

One of the most common lessons I have encountered in leadership is the notion that one should lead by example. Searching for its origin, I found it is mentioned in the creed of Navy SEALS. The famous Chinese military general Sun Tzu is also a proponent of leading by example (versus, by force). Being hands-on and "walking the walk" are essential aspects of leadership, but without a mission, readiness and the willingness to perform these are inert.

My nineteenth birthday was spent at Lackland Air Force Base in Texas, where I was most of the way through Basic Training, about ready to begin Tech School. I have a memory of receiving my Orders – an official piece of paper indicating that on a certain date, I would travel to Chanute Air Force Base in Illinois to begin my next round of training.

So often in my career, I have received Orders from a company, where the notions of mission and vision are conspicuously absent. Even in larger organizations, it is surprisingly rare to have the company's mission or its vision discussed as a component of how an action will be carried out. While we are almost always task-oriented, and while there is usually a right way and a wrong way for a task to be completed, one's overall mission at any time – which again, is a key component of leadership – can be as vague as, "do a good job," or worse, "do what you are told."

In situations like this, you already have an advantage in leadership, based on all the work we have completed together. From the discussions about reputation and ethics, to exploring your personal brand, hopefully you have some sense of what you want to achieve in your life that is bigger than the tasks you might be given to do, or the Orders of the day.

Perhaps you will be lucky enough in your career to land the opportunity to work with a company or a non-profit where the mission and vision provide practical guidance to your tasks. For example, if you work for the Patagonia Company, you will help create superior products while avoiding harm, as part of a venture committed to introducing environmentally friendly solutions.[1] Also consider the mission of the John D. and Catherine T. MacArthur Foundation, which is vehemently "committed to building a more just, verdant and peaceful world."[2] Not only do mission statements provide guidance for day-to-day activities, they can become so well known that much of the public's knowledge of these entities is built upon these foundations, having to do with their unique values and operating guidelines.

With missions like these established and actively discussed, what it means to guide these entities forward (leadership) and direct them skillfully (management) is self-evident. Another measure of how clear, practical missions like these make organizations more successful is to notice how obvious failure would be. If employees at Patagonia build inferior products or do something that harms the environment, they are on the wrong track, and one would expect the employees, management systems and leaders to leap into corrective action.

If you are seeking to work with those who set themselves apart as extraordinary leaders, start by looking for companies with excellent reputations, where the principals lead by example, and where the missions and visions are so practical and integral that they inspire you to do great work. If the company's overall purpose does not inspire you on its own, it should at least allow you to advance your career objectives.

Sign 2 of Successful Leadership: Strong Culture

I have had excellent luck engaging with the owners of companies that attract a lot of talent, and fortunately, that phenomenon is holding steady. Any number of factors can produce the spark that draws the applicants ... but often it is as simple as having a prominent project come to life. Leviathan experienced this when musical artist Amon Tobin enlisted it as part of the team to design his ISAM Live show, which was written about in the *WIRED* magazine. To this day, that project opens doors for Leviathan and makes cutting-edge talents want to work there.

Producing a buzz-worthy project that captures global attention is obviously not the same skill set as building a company culture where people seek to work and stay throughout their careers. Certainly, it is a good idea to investigate the longevity of the management team and the key leaders in any given company. I also recommend looking at the newest additions, and those at the entry level, to see how they are feeling about their career opportunities.

To offer up a company with a constructive culture which translates into overall workplace consciousness, Cutters Studios is a prime example. The employees at all levels refer to the day-to-day business relationships with their colleagues as being family-like, and most of their clients are on the exact same page, regularly professing their love for the company's people and culture at every opportunity. As I have seen first-hand, it has much to do with the dedication to customer service and extraordinary craftsmanship, but also, to appreciation for life itself and a commitment to treating everyone like a VIP. At Cutters Studios, that certainly applies to the clients, but notably, to the interns as well.

Back in 2007, my client company ATTIK was acquired by Dentsu, and six years later, Dentsu also purchased Mitchell Communications Group, an extraordinarily successful PR firm billing U.S. $11 million annually, with 75 full-time employees and offices in 14 states across America.[3] These developments led to a call in 2013 where Mitchell's CEO Elise Mitchell introduced herself and sounded me out on my work for ATTIK. In her 2017 book entitled *Leading through the Turn*, Ms. Mitchell provides some fascinating insights into her journey. Through her stories, we come to understand how leaving her job in Memphis as a director of corporate communications for Promus Hotels and relocating to Arkansas prompted her to start her own agency. From landing Promus as her first client in 1995, to arriving at various crossroads and making the necessary strategic decisions along the way, she reveals the critical thinking she used to plot her course.

In her chapter called "Defining a Destiny," Ms. Mitchell articulates the importance of the strong, supportive work environment she and her colleagues instilled through various means. Despite the rich rewards in store for high-caliber PR professionals when they move to new companies, Ms. Mitchell attributed her company's above-average retention rate to its positive culture.[4]

The Blake Project is a Los Angeles-based brand consultancy helping companies design, manage, and build brands that drive profitable revenue growth through differentiated customer experiences. The group also regularly stages Brand Positioning Workshops, and its principals share their considerable knowledge through their Branding Strategy Insider blog and newsletter. Here is the overview for the group's Brand Culture Workshop.

- We believe that a key component to a brand's success lies in forging a rich culture/ecosystem/community that people feel they belong to and that they actively advocate to others. Powerful brand cultures are built from the interaction of a range of elements: A strong sense of purpose, emanating from your mission, vision, and values, that helps you build brand equity by enabling your brand to stand for an idea that people want to celebrate every day; clear storylines that give the brand a unified sense of direction, but that can also be segmented by audience; experiences that bring people together and enable them to share being part of the community.[5]

The groundbreaking *The Design of Business*, from Roger Martin, who is widely acclaimed as one of the world's most influential minds in management and global business, is another amazing reference on this subject. Well before the book was published in 2009, Mr. Martin had privileged access to the principals of Research in Motion Limited, the company that now operates under the name of the once-ubiquitous device that ushered us into the smartphone era: Blackberry. Having once achieved a market value of over U.S. $80 billion, the accounts drawn first-hand from RIM's founder and "design visionary" Mike Laziridis are extraordinary. To put them into context, it is helpful to have some understanding of Mr. Martin's illuminating framework of the design of business. We will return to his ideas in the context of our ongoing discussion soon, so here is a primer.[6]

> The design thinker therefore enables the organization to balance exploration and exploitation, invention of business and administration of business, and originality and mastery. Design thinking powers the design of business, the directed movement of a business through the knowledge funnel from mystery to heuristic to algorithm and then the utilization of the efficiencies to tackle the next mystery and the next and the next. The velocity of movement through the knowledge funnel, powered by design thinking, is the most powerful formula for competitive advantage in the twenty-first century.

This passage, appearing on page 26 of Mr. Martin's book, contains language you may be unfamiliar with in this context. To decode it, you can read the first part of the book, or you can just bear with me as we forge ahead. In my understanding, what he is describing are phenomena that apply to every business I can imagine, where the key is finding a balance between good, solid business management practices, and innovation.

Based on these ideas, I am hoping these comments from Mr. Laziridis included later in Mr. Martin's narrative will inspire you. "In a business," he is quoted as saying,

> "no matter how good the process is, no matter how much you've got it down pat, no matter how much money you are making, how efficient, you have to always go back and say, 'Is there something fundamentally wrong with the way we are seeing the market? Are we dealing with incomplete information?'"[7]

When you package the mindsets from these gentlemen with Ms. Mitchell's, and think about the values that come from having a strong mission which is practical and integral, you then have the critical ingredients necessary to provide what people generally want from an employer. According to Ms. Mitchell and a 2014 survey of 15,000 millennial college students she cites in her book, here is what those wise young people seek, in priority order: Cultural fit; career opportunities; lifestyle synergy; pay/benefits.[8]

Sign 3 of Successful Leadership: Opportunities Abound

If you live in a rural area and there are very few employers, that has traditionally been a legitimate career obstacle. Welcome to the new era, where a skilled communications consultant has every opportunity to thrive, even living in a ghost town.

A few years ago, I attended a business development workshop for creative agencies in Nashville, hosted by two very smart individuals. The first is David C. Baker, the principal of the management consulting firm ReCourses, and a highly accomplished publisher and author. His colleague Blair Enns, author of *The Win without Pitching Manifesto* and *Pricing Creativity*, was the co-leader of the event. Over the past decade, Mr. Enns has established himself as one of the world's leading authorities on new business for creative agencies and freelancers, and one main aspect of his business is travelling to speak with agencies and at business conferences. It is safe to say that there is nothing in this book that is unfamiliar to Mr. Enns; asserting his expertise on most of this subject matter is a good way for me to underscore how much knowledge and proficiency goes into having true expertise in sales.

Now, imagine Mr. Enns standing in front of a group of successful businesspeople who have paid to bring him in. Bear in mind that most attendees are well familiar with his books. Generally, he has already positioned himself by the time he steps before such a crowd. One thing I remember him telling us from the stage in Nashville was that he lives in a very remote area in Canada, where he is certain that there are zero potential clients living anywhere near him. To this, he added a helpful theorem, strongly suggesting that properly defining one's expertise through positioning makes it easy to identify one's target audience.[9]

In the larger business world where companies like international design and consulting firm IDEO operate, the design thinking framework affects leadership and culture, while also underwriting a multitude of communications opportunities (for research, assessment, reporting, analysis, etc.). For this reason, I wanted to ensure you are familiar enough with the concept to alert you: Anywhere design thinking is a topic of discussion has a high potential for being a trail worth following as a communications consultant.

To create value for our clients, we must find and illuminate information that will help a company succeed in the future. Where innovation is occurring, or where we can nurture it, being able to turn that information to advantage, while building on the day-to-day company foundation in a way that bolsters it strengths, is exactly what a successful communications consultant achieves.

In the language of design thinking, communicators are essential in helping a company harvest its exploitation (the fruits it gathers from its day-to-day operations) and its exploration (research and renewal efforts), achieve better balance between both realms, and succeed.

Of course, the key ingredients we want to identify in potential clients are not always present. Can you imagine anyone not wanting to work for Research in Motion during the boom-era of the Blackberry? Although the company remains tremendously successful, the fact that nearly 16,000 employees lost their jobs over six years casts a harsh light. A 2015 story published in Canadian Business entitled "The inside story of how the wheels came off at Research in Motion" cites numerous weaknesses. Among those mentioned are quality-control issues, managerial gridlock – and what might be described as a lack of a common mission and vision from the company's leaders that was practical and integral.

Closer to home, with my focus on working with relatively small companies, I have been onboard for more than one crash. Certainly, there were warning signs: the leadership wavered; the orders became unclear or nonexistent; and/or the checks were delayed. I would guess that any of those 16,000 former Research in Motion staffers could describe registering similar clues well before their pink slips arrived. Despite obvious warning signs, rather than quitting when the going gets tough, many of us instinctively demonstrate the highly valued traits of optimism, persistence, and perseverance. Unfortunately, like some marriages, those who enter business together sometimes grow apart, despite everyone's best efforts. Also worth noting, for design thinkers, a commitment to innovation can lead to legitimate needs to pivot, and even to full-on paradigm shifts.

With these truths in mind, here is some overriding advice: When you are sure of what you do and how you do it, if you find a business or a client where opportunities abound for you to apply yourself, that is an excellent place to start. And again, if the vision and mission factor in and inspire you, and the culture is attractive, I encourage you to climb aboard, if you can.

Sign 4 of Successful Leadership: Fit

As noted, in their job searches, millennial college students prioritize cultural fit. That summation offers insight into the critical importance of the liaison you are subject to working with.

The stories shared here about businesses growing convey a common progression. Mrs. Mitchell attributes this phenomenon to the science behind the Greiner Curve, named after University of Southern California management and organization professor Larry Greiner. As you can see, companies tend to grow and experience problems so consistently that they all fall into one of six specific stages or "crises."[10] These stages well understood, and Mr. Greiner's research has long been able to demonstrate the critical management frameworks necessary to overcome them.

Obviously, there is a lot more to know about precisely what the Greiner Curve maps, and where any given company might fall on the chart. I share it here to help you see the variations – and the constancy of change – in life and business. Trying to determine where a company's leaders are in dealing with change can help you understand how well you are likely to fit in over time. In turn, that information can – and probably should – be a factor in determining whether you pursue opportunities there.

To tie all this together, let's consider the signs of leadership in the specialized creative agency Leviathan, over time. When I first met the company's president in 2011, he was confident about his venture bringing something new to the business world, largely skewing into the realm of experiential marketing and the creation of premium digital content and interactive installations.

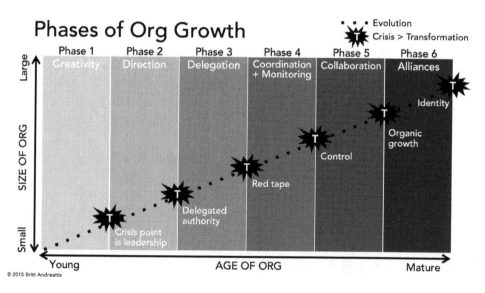

Figure 2 Greiner's Model Curve. Andreatta, B. (2018, September 7). *Nurture and Anticipate Growth with the Greiner Curve*. BrittAndreatta.Com. https://www.brittandreatta.com/nurture-and-anticipate-growth-with-the-greiner-curve-1-in-3-part-series/ [11]

The introduction I received became a mission when I was engaged to serve its clear PR objectives. Having worked with some similar companies fusing production, interactive and "show business" for events and installations – and having enjoyed that work – by the time I sent my proposal, I had a strong sense of the company's vision, its culture, the opportunities, and how I would fit in. We have had an excellent run together over many years, despite experiencing some challenges at times. Through them all, my work has been treated as a critical part of the management framework that has kept things moving forward on a positive trajectory.

Leviathan is the third DWA client to be acquired by another business entity during my tenure. In the first instance with ATTIK, there was a long transition period, where the owners kept me onboard. With Leviathan, I was paused almost instantly, invited back onboard for an extended engagement within a few months, then reinstated during the 2020 pandemic.

To me, all of this provides lasting evidence for validating the best signs of leadership in a potential client company. We can also use another measure I suggested for you, which is to assess how working with a company can allow you to serve your own career objectives. In hindsight, mine have soared to new heights through my work with Leviathan, and through all my esteemed clients, past and present.

Exploration

1. List four living business luminaries you would love to work for. What are their key characteristics or achievements that are most attractive to you?
2. Research three companies you are interested in working with, and write out their missions. Which one inspires you the most, and why?
3. Recalling your own career objectives, do any leaders or companies seem like perfect fits as employers or clients? If so, list the top five.
4. List pros and cons – five apiece – for working with a company that has just brought in a new marketing leader.
5. What valuable takeaways would you expect from asking a company's receptionist about its culture?
6. How can design thinking help the simplest business – like a lemonade stand – be more competitive?
7. Regarding employment or contracting, do you agree that cultural fit is more important than work/life balance and compensation? Explain your point of view. Whether employed or contracted, is there any difference?
8. What is the best example of a positive corporate culture you have experienced, and what made it special?

9. Perhaps one of the best ways to find job opportunities that are a fit for your expertise is to search job listings. See if you can find five job listings that seem perfect for you, even if they are full or part time, or based outside of your region. Can you imagine a way to introduce yourself to the executives behind those job postings and ask them to consider you as a remote employee or outside contractor?
10. List four other ways you can identify positions that are a good fit for you, in the absence of a published job listing.

Notes

1 Our Core Values - Patagonia. (n.d.). Patagonia.com. Retrieved February 26, 2021, from https://www.patagonia.com/core-values/.
2 About. (n.d.). MacArthur Foundation. Retrieved February 26, 2021, from https://www.macfound.org/about/.
3 Stein, L. (2015, November 18). Dentsu Acquires Mitchell as It Enters PR Space. *PR Week*. http://bit.ly/Z2pKsj.
4 Mitchell, E. (2016). *Leading Through the Turn: How a Journey Mindset Can Help Leaders Find Success and Significance* (1st ed.). McGraw-Hill Education.
5 Daye, D. (2020, June 2). Brand Culture Workshop. *Branding Strategy Insider*. https://www.brandingstrategyinsider.com/brand-culture-workshop/.
6 Martin, R.L. (2009). *The Design of Business: Why Design Thinking Is the Next Competitive Advantage* (3rd ed.). Harvard Business Review Press.
7 Ibid.
8 Mitchell, E. (2016). *Leading Through the Turn: How a Journey Mindset Can Help Leaders Find Success and Significance* (1st ed.). McGraw-Hill Education.
9 Enns, B. (2020, December 3). Ten Tests of Your Positioning. *Win Without Pitching*. http://bit.ly/wwp10t.
10 Petrone, P. (2016, December 2). Greiner Curve, 6 Stages Organizations Goes Through as They Mature. *LinkedIn*. http://bit.ly/Gcurve.
11 Andreatta, B. (2018, September 7). Nurture and Anticipate Growth with the Greiner Curve. *BrittAndreatta.com*. http://bit.ly/2wUT5yC.

6
Objectives

Beyond the leadership strengths of your potential clients, the precise ways in which their missions and visions translate into action have everything to do with their objectives. We have discussed this fateful concept many times up until now. In conversations about my job and how it applies to others, I will often say something like, "Understanding what public relations involves can be confusing, so to boil it down, I always begin by talking about objectives. What is it you are wanting to accomplish, and why?" Once those questions are answered and prioritized in our To-Do list, we then can devise our strategies ... then move into tactics aimed toward achieving our desired results in the best ways possible.

We have also focused on the importance of strategy and its application. As we have seen, in the exploration of personal branding, when framing the work to be done and the problems to be resolved, everything starts with objectives. Hearing this from a person whose first consulting business card stated, "Objectives Strategies Results" along with his company name, phone number and tag line, "Dynamic public relations," hopefully you are getting a strong sense of how communications consulting works, and the common roots for effective, strategic plans of action.

Types of Objectives

Another way of thinking and talking about business objectives is to frame the discussion according to needs. If a businessperson you are speaking with does not clarify a specific challenge or difficulty being faced, it seems unlikely that discussion will lead to a business relationship. Not too long ago, I attended an open house for a successful entrepreneur here in Asheville, and as we got to know each other, right away, a few things came up that provided potential for collaboration. Their two-person shop had gotten so busy that

DOI: 10.4324/9781003177951-6

they could rarely even answer the phone. Also, they have a good reputation locally, but the desire to expand that further in the region and nationally was expressed. For the first predicament, I shared an idea about establishing an internship program with a local university, where the program could provide some marketing training. If all went well, their energetic intern would be able to field inbound inquiries and contribute to a proactive social media campaign, which could raise the company's online profile. To summarize, I left that 30-minute conversation with two potential objectives for this local business.

1. Address manpower shortage to better equip company for fielding marketing inquiries.
2. Increase effort and focus on communicating company's stories and strengths through social media – and potentially, through media relations – to reach a larger audience.

From my point of view, I am confident that every business has an obvious need in one or more of these areas, at any given time: profitability; sales and marketing; customer service; leadership; hiring and retention; brand strategy; growth; financial management; productivity; logistics. Any serious need in one area is likely to affect several others. For example, in a scenario where an important employee leaves for a new job, that can be a wake-up call for management to realize they need to focus better on retention, all while attracting and training a replacement. Customer service, productivity, profitability, and marketing are a few areas that might easily be impacted by the departure of a single essential employee. If it is a manager or top-level executive, the impact is sure to be even greater.

Another sharp article I want to share on this subject comes from business management and turnaround consultant Dan Feliciano. His references are also highly impressive: He cites the groundbreaking 1992 article, "The Balanced Scorecard: Measures That Drive Performance," published in *Harvard Business Review* by authors Robert Kaplan and David Norton, as well as their subsequent publications; the work of Jay Barney and Ricky Griffin in their widely referenced book, *The Management of Organizations*; and a study/article published in American Psychologist from professors Edwin Locke and Gary Latham, entitled "Building a Practically Useful Theory of Goal Setting and Task Motivation – A 35-Year Odyssey."

Mr. Feliciano's article, published in Fast Company back in 2008, stands atop the shoulders of these illustrious thought leaders, to deliver this informed conclusion: To be productive and feel secure, employees must know what is expected of them, why their work is important, the standards of performance, and how they measure up to those standards.[1]

This is a powerful, insightful takeaway from a treasure trove of scientific research into management and human motivation. Can you extrapolate some organizational objectives from it? Maybe:

1. Establish a training program to ensure employees understand the particulars of their job function, how that fits within the company's mission, and the impact of their performance.
2. Establish and encourage the use of communications channels where employees share ideas and concerns, to provide regular feedback and stimulate personal growth and job satisfaction.

These two objectives could potentially apply to any company you might work with, helping to meet the needs of employees and improve its chances for providing an attractive, healthy workplace. To a business leader aiming to succeed, what are those benefits worth? The answer will depend on whether any of the other types of objectives listed by Mr. Root are demanding attention. When all is well, it is reasonable to expect that actively, effectively attending to ideas like these would be considered mission critical; and yet, attempting to prevent a disruption, or trying to clean up after one, often top a company's list of needs from one day to the next. Indeed, forestalling a crisis or recovering from one very well may be the reason a company needs to hire you.

From imagining a company experiencing a rough patch and that providing your opening, I want to look in the opposite direction, where the entrepreneur is building an organization around innovation. When I encountered research presented by OpenText promoting the benefits of delivering the Continuous Connected Customer Journey, it got my attention.

- Customer Engagement has overtaken cost and risk reduction as the primary business objective. Customer engagement technology is now connecting organizations with the customer journey by providing relevant, personalized, and timely information in each point of interaction.[2]

This information illuminates the importance of objectives in the companies we work with. Some might be caught up in extinguishing fires, while others might be building a business of the future. Depending upon your own interests – and certainly, your assessments of the people at any given company you are considering building a connection with – you might find the most affinity with one on either end of this spectrum, or somewhere in between.

Even for companies stuck in crisis-management mode, your knowledge of proven management intelligence and methodologies that can be applied to better motivate employees – for example, or to help lead a company toward the future by updating its processes, with customer needs in mind – can make you a highly trusted and extremely valuable member of any team. Therefore, I encourage you to dig deeper into all the references provided above, whenever time allows. With that in mind, here is a link to a more in-depth discussion of Kaplan and Norton's Balanced Scorecard, where you can also download a template to help you translate mission and vision into suitable actions.

- Balanced Scorecard: https://www.toolshero.com/strategy/balanced-scorecard/

To effectively put the Balanced Scorecard to use, you may also want to investigate this article to better understand the authors' use of the term <u>measures</u>: "The Balanced Scorecard: Measures that Drive Performance."[3] My interpretation is, measures are what we use to determine the quality of performance against our goals. One might be, how many employees has a company lost this year?

Objective-Driven Communications Showcase

I spent a little time thinking about the objectives that have been put in front of me in my client engagements over the years. The desire to appear in the *WIRED* magazine is now standard, although when I worked with The Terpin Group, everyone wanted to be in the *Wall Street Journal*. Other major client motivations are sometimes a little more difficult to gather, but there are several safe bets. In my experience, companies usually want their reputations to precede them. Also, while a company may be creative and masterful at storytelling for its clients, following the familiar notion of the cobbler's children having no shoes, very often a company does not apply its talents to masterfully conveying its own story. Here are a few more examples from my journey to-date serving the communications needs of some stellar individuals and businesses.

In 2003, when I started what turned into an 11-year run as PR counsel for global creative agency ATTIK, my eyes were wide open, since I had engaged with the company back in 2000 and resigned the account just a few weeks later. Briefly, when we partnered up initially, the firm had several communications professionals onboard to serve its different offices; when I left, my advice was for them to just focus on communicating well with the incumbent in NYC. A few years later, the door reopened, and by then, I had moved across the country, a recession had rocked the global economy, ATTIK had restructured and achieved something miraculous, and I was thrilled to reconnect with them.

Through our collaborations in 2000, we spoke about the firm as "the leading all-media creative solutions provider." By then, ATTIK already had a 14-year history, and while it had come a long way from its roots in northern England where the founders' ambitious efforts put them on the map as a source for sensational graphic design – strongly rooted in branding – in retrospect, the company's instability seems to have come from focusing mostly on projects, rather than relationships. In 2003, winning Toyota's youth-targeted Scion brand as its first-ever Agency of Record account was a keystone in catapulting ATTIK to the coveted position of "global creative agency." The period between 2000 and 2003 described above was full of anguish and difficulty for ATTIK's partners, and yet it had a happy ending that included the company being acquired many years later.

You might be surprised to know how many creative industry entrepreneurs I have met over the years who have referred to ATTIK's story as one they admire. In fact, I once had a potential client's growth objectives expressed to me like so: "We see ourselves on a trajectory that's similar to ATTIK." Did I win that account? You bet I did. Helping companies move from handling projects through agencies to handling accounts as agencies is a proven aspect of my expertise. Therefore, for any company aspiring to achieve an "ATTIK Trajectory," my experience as ATTIK's PR counsel over a meteoric 11-year period is potent.

I want to share a few more examples of overt company objectives where I have seen impressive results. One is from the Elise Mitchell, who built up her PR consultancy to such a magnificent level and degree that she was able to sell it to Dentsu. Reading her book provides a fascinating look into how one might take an interest in communications, couple that with the particulars of her existence, and then build something so much more successful than most people can imagine. Here are three more initiatives from companies I have worked with, where the impacts on each have been massive. For the record, these developments pre-dated my relationships with each of these companies, although they all established new ventures that opened phenomenal opportunities for me.

In Chicago, Michael Shapiro started his theatrical staging and exhibit fabrication company Ravenswood Studio in 1989. Beginning with just 1,000 square feet of space, within 18 years, its space grew to 60,000 square feet. A couple of years before reaching 100,000 square feet in 2013, Mr. Shapiro and his colleagues hatched a very strategic idea. Within their walls, as a sister company to Ravenswood, they formed Luci Creative in 2011, as a planning, strategy and design firm targeting cultural and corporate clients. Having learned so much about the business environment in which their company operated, and seen many projects lost to or controlled by companies like Luci, these entrepreneurs took a big gamble on incubating a new entity that could operate higher on the food chain, and thereby benefit the original company. Luci's achievements have been consistently remarkable, and without its existence, it seems probable that many of Ravenswood's best projects would have gone to one of its competitors.

America's "second city" is also the headquarters for Cutters Studios, which launched there in 1980 as commercial editorial company Cutters. Operating at an extremely high level over the years, while also seeing how other similar businesses were adapting to maximize economic opportunities, CEO Tim McGuire and his partners started growing. After opening Cutters in Los Angeles and New York, he also added related capabilities, and shrewdly branded them. As a result, over time, along came Another Country as a premier audio house, a live-action production division named Dictionary Films, and a design, animation and finishing business named SOL Design FX.

Fast forward several years to 2013, when Mr. McGuire and his partners learned about the demise of a company that had been doing extremely well in the space where SOL operated. At its height, the company Superfad was consistently winning high-profile projects and creative industry awards through its offices in Seattle, LA, and New York. When the operation folded, that left a lot of very accomplished talents out of work. Among them were former Superfad LA Executive Creative Director Brad Tucker and Executive Producer Darren Jaffe. In short, the Cutters Studios executives jumped at the opportunity to hire Tucker and Jaffe for SOL Design FX ... but Tucker took a stand: To him, he felt that the Cutters Studios design division needed a sexier name. In the end, Cutters did not just add two new hires in LA; by adopting the new name of "Flavor" and a new brand presence for its design division, it raised its international profile and made positive impacts for its operations across America.

And since Tucker and Jaffe were friends of mine, my professional introduction to the Cutters family also was due to them – as were the company-wide promotional objectives brought to the forefront through their contagious ambitions.

Exploration

1. Think about "what you are wanting to accomplish, and why." Name four ways in which applying yourself as a communications consultant to those needs can impact them.
2. In considering becoming a communications consultant, you probably have a potential client in mind. Which of the Ten Most Important Business Objectives introduced by Mr. Root do you feel are most relevant to that client? How would you begin to address them based on what you know?
3. List five benefits of establishing a marketing internship program for a client company. Also, list five benefits for the intern(s).
4. Studies show that employee motivation increases when they know what, why and how to do something, and when they understand how well they are performing. How would you convince a company executive to account for these employee needs when they are not accounted for?
5. In your opinion, what are the top five benefits of a company with a happy workforce?
6. List three examples of companies you are aware of that you feel are demonstrating a successful "Customer Engagement" strategy using technology.
7. List three examples of companies you are aware of that you feel do not have a successful "Customer Engagement" strategy using technology, but that should.
8. Download a copy of the Balanced Scorecard template using the link provided in this chapter and complete it for your own business.
9. List four "measures" that you feel are likely to be important to any company you would want to work for. Two examples would be, having internal communication channels in alignment, and ensuring those channels are actively used to reflect the day-to-day happenings at a given company.
10. List two different "objective-driven communications initiatives" that have come to your attention from any business and include details on how you know about each one.

Notes

1 Feliciano, D. (2008, April 9). Why Are Goals and Objectives Important? *Fast Company*. http://bit.ly/DFgoals.

2 How to deliver a connected customer journey - eBook. (2017, November 24). *OpenText*. https://www.opentext.com/info/experience-suite.
3 Kaplan, R.S., & Norton, D.P. (1992, January 1). The Balanced Scorecard—Measures that Drive Performance. *Harvard Business Review*. http://bit.ly/KNmeasure.

7
Business Brands and Branding

The same concepts, diligence, and approaches that apply to building and solidifying personal brands represent the framework for successfully developing and leveraging corporate brands. There would certainly be value in going play-by-play through the earlier chapters' guidelines and addressing the corporate variations, given the complications – and improvements – that can arise when efforts are elevated to higher levels, and exposed to greater numbers of experts. Instead, to make things more interesting, I am going to leap directly into showcasing some wondrous branding feats. Many of these examples come straight from my personal experiences, where I have been immersed in highly sophisticated branding practices and discovered some very novel paths to winning in business.

Most top-level business executives share an appreciation for branding. Of course, since there are infinite examples of poor or awful branding for every good one – there are also plenty of skeptics. Before commencing, think about your interest level in the distillation of a company's identity into strategically apt symbols, positioning statements, color schemes, and communications elements. The following exploration has solid potential for lifting your knowledge and expertise in realms that are vastly important to virtually every business under the sun: If all of this stirs your passions, that is a good sign.

Why Brand?

Searching to find definitive insights into what is of critical importance to understand about brands, there are a lot of voices to filter. For my taste, I am drawn to insights provided by Scott Goodson, the founder of agency StrawberryFrog and the author of the book *Uprising* from McGraw Hill, in a May 2012 article he published in *Forbes*.[1] Among the unique powers and propensities he attributes to brands – including representing reputations, and connections to customers – he addresses the importance of what we

DOI: 10.4324/9781003177951-7

covered regarding personal brands: differentiation. With distinction being key to a company's financial success, he also reveres brands' abilities to drive behavior.

Around the time Mr. Goodson's article appeared, author, speaker, and ghostwriter Jeff Haden had interviewed David C. Baker of ReCourses.[2] Mr. Baker provided an elegant summation of effective branding and storytelling. My takeaway is this: For outsiders, branding plays a part in conveying what is true about a company; by using honest storytelling, those attributes can meaningfully take life and build equity. For all elements to exist harmoniously and produce the desired results, they must be aligned, and truthful.

That focus once again returns us to this point in our exploration of personal branding: Even at the highest levels, finding what is unique about a brand compared to its competitors is a key in what becomes its simplified brand identity at the core of its communications. According to Mr. Baker, the summation, and the execution all must ring true – and be "in alignment" – to be effective over time.

Now, let's sample some other voices. In a world-famous TED Talk, author and speaker Simon Sinek invokes the examples of Apple, Martin Luther King, Jr., and the Wright brothers to help us understand that the best way to establish our uniqueness for the purpose of inspiring others is to "start with why" – or in other words, to root all communications by explaining the core of our belief system.[3] While I find his premise to be highly intelligent and enlightening, consultant and entrepreneur Yonatan Kagansky argues a great counterpoint in his 2018 article published on *Hacker Noon* entitled, "Don't Start with Why!"[4] Building his case by acknowledging the power of missions while clarifying that talking about them does not constitute the key to business success, Mr. Kagansky embraces great storytelling as the true secret behind the world's most influential marketing model.

In summary, brands are established to differentiate companies and their products in their marketplaces. To do so effectively, there must be deep understanding of every aspect of its existence, from the personalities of its principals to their common mission, and naturally, the essential details of its products, services, and operations. With a fitting, honest and accurate brand that is aligned to all corporate beliefs and values, storytelling and marketing can be applied to engage the audiences the brand is intended to serve and support. In the absence of having a well-defined brand, the storytelling and marketing have no hero. Therefore, designing or solidifying a brand's identity is a highly intelligent first step in building a business, or in taking its success to new heights.

Brand Creation and Development

Step by step, this book's chapter on Personal Brands and Branding explains some common methodologies you will find at the heart of developing any brand systematically. Among those are the POSTAR model often used in instructional systems design, where moving through a framework of Positioning, Objectives, Strategies, Tactics, Administration, and Results – and then being prepared to repeat that cycle as necessary over time – allows us to proceed from research through strategic planning and into action, logically and effectively. Through my experiences with the U.S. Air Force, the similar framework I learned to use is called ADDIE (Analysis, Design, Development, Implementation, Evaluation).

The objectives for brand development and creation are to strategically distill the entity's core values – including internal and external ones – resolving the visual, aural, and even cultural representations into something unique, recognizable and (ideally) relatively simple. In the best cases, as you will see, the result is something that comes about after all the POSTAR or ADDIE due diligence has taken place, and the solution is elegant, brilliant, and simple, while remaining open to change and new influences over time.

Introducing his interview of Mr. Baker, Mr. Haden mentions that others' experiences represent the true bottom line in any brand's meaning. For the likes of a Pepsi or Coca-Cola, it is easy to see the truth in that assessment. At the same time, since both of those companies are so proactive with their advertising and marketing efforts, the roles strategic communications play in shaping perceptions are also readily apparent.

Mr. Baker's most critical assessments of branding and storytelling target those who fail to go about these vital communications facets correctly. To help you understand how to avoid those pitfalls, I will delve into several examples of brand development that have proven to be successful, shining some light on the diligent approaches behind specific instances of brand development. We will first review situations where the brand was unknown, then proceed into the realm where the owners decided the time had come for a rebrand ... or at least, a refresh.

Building Brands from Scratch

Based in Irvine, California, the principals of the design and innovation consultancy ENVOY have built their company very thoughtfully, aiming to partner with bold leaders to make experiences and products that define the future. By focusing on the convergence of design and technology, and even being willing to invest capital, expertise and services, the agency has chosen to engage with a growing list of innovative startups, in addition to its roster of well-established companies.

When we think about startups, we might imagine one or two impassioned individuals burning the midnight oil together in a garage or an attic, dreaming about taking their side gig full-time. This is a story about the other kind – where very savvy professionals who have achieved major success in the past join forces on a relatively sure thing. Meet Blossom, a company that set out to create a smart water controller that would cut utility bills and save water. One of the most successful companies to tap into the "Internet of Things" phenomenon (essentially, where our electronic devices can send and receive data and adjust themselves according to what they learn) in 2014, Blossom's accomplished founders counted dozens of prior patent filings between them. By the time they met ENVOY in 2013, they already had financial backing from Vizio and Accton, and the mission was leveraging their experiences in consumer electronics, water resources, networking, and hardware to deliver innovative, impactful products.

Going into November 2014, the scope of services ENVOY had provided to Blossom's executive team included the company name, its logo, a complete brand identity that included positioning and guidelines, a website, mobile app design and development, industrial design for the product, and strategy and execution for the product's launch – and promotion, through the company's channels, networks, and resources – via a Kickstarter pre-order campaign. After meeting its initial U.S. $30,000 fundraising goal in less than 24 hours, the campaign went on to raise over U.S. $100,000.[5] Two years later, Blossom was acquired by Scott's Miracle-Gro.[6]

There is a lot to learn from this magnificent case study. First, ENVOY's own brand, mission, and positioning were so well established that when Blossom's executives came along, they knew it was a perfect fit. For any new venture seeking to go to market in a powerful way, bring strengths to the surface and ensure the greatest chances for success, the partnership between ENVOY and Blossom is a solid example of how all that is done at an extremely high level.

My introduction of a marketing consultancy as a brand – one that has established expertise in creating or invigorating the brands of others – is intentional here. To attract the principals and investors behind Blossom, ENVOY had to be perceived as being worthy. The agency's internal focus and the expertise it represented for others had to be applied in creating its own identity, and in telling its own story. The proof of ENVOY's own successful branding campaign is evident in the Blossom case study, which is yet another example of a powerful, extremely well-engineered brand, shrewdly taken to market with tightly aligned, highly engaging storytelling.

Now, let's look at another agency that set out on the path to help others engineer their brands for success. Back in 1986 in Northern England, Batley School of Art students James Sommerville and Simon Needham used a £2,000 grant from His Royal Highness the Prince of Wales to set up a new venture in the unused attic of Sommerville's grandmother. This is the well-known origin story for ATTIK, which in 2007 was acquired by Dentsu, the world's largest advertising agency brand. Announcing the acquisition, Dentsu listed ATTIK's clients as Adidas, Boost Mobile, Coca-Cola, Heineken, Lexus, and Toyota Motor Sales USA's Scion brand ... citing 58 employees and billings of U.S. $80 million.[7]

Over time, ATTIK became famous for its fierce dedication to design and to brands, where its work leveraged every marketing channel, and integrated traditional and non-traditional practices to forever alter the automotive marketing industry. It is worth noting that the firm's early days in England were pre-Internet. The enterprising young men knew that success would require more than talent and a catchy name, and they shrewdly decided to self-publish an ambitious, collectible printed piece that would set the creative bar as high as possible. Hoping to attract higher caliber work, clients, and collaborators, they set about researching and exploring all their ideas, working after hours and on weekends to bring their best conceptions to life in print at any cost. That project, which eventually came to be known as Noise, paid some extraordinary dividends: Over the years, Needham often acknowledged how the commitment to publishing Noise continuously drove ATTIK's work and its outlook to the cutting edge. Further, Noise is credited with helping the firm attract its best opportunities.

Between 1993 and 2009, ATTIK published five Noise editions, and each is acclaimed for breaking new ground in its era. Meanwhile, behind the scenes, the growing global collective of creative problem-solvers continued to create advertising, design, and interactive experiences that got the world talking, pointing, staring, blogging, and remembering its clients' brands. Deeply rooted in brand-engineering and creativity throughout its life, ATTIK's story inspired millions, which is a legacy for Mr. Needham, Mr. Sommerville, and partners including Will Travis and Ric Peralta. The venture met its end in 2015, when Dentsu laid it to rest.[8]

There is another extremely powerful ingredient in ATTIK's story: Over time, the co-founders consistently credited their ethos for attracting extraordinary clients and talents. Certainly, by the time it hit 200 employees, the company's pitch as a global ideas company providing unique communication solutions for the world's most exciting and innovative brands was highly polished. Another unique selling proposition focused on strategic thinking based on insights. In the introduction to the company's 1999-era Credentials document (yet another groundbreaking, over-sized, highly ambitious print piece), Mr. Needham waxed sentimental about the vital role of a strong brand in the effectiveness of communications. The point is this: Even if something is incredibly creative, audiences will not follow a weak brand.

The term ethos is used to define the essence of a culture, or the mindset and other ties that draw and hold individuals together. For ATTIK, the hundreds of talents attracted to staff positions, and the thousands who worked on agency projects, were inspired to be part of excellent communications that positively set the client brands apart ... the same way ATTIK positively set itself apart.

Here are a few of the assignments ATTIK earned to formally introduce new brands to the world.

In 2010, the world-famous art book publisher TASCHEN Books released *Brand Identity Now*, written by its longstanding design editor, Julius Wiedemann. Including ATTIK's work in the book, Mr. Wiedemann called out its rare ability to incorporate beauty alongside usability. Commenting on how openness and elegance – in the right measures – can improve the world, he cited ATTIK as masters of that intricate communications balancing act.

Each of the brands mentioned in ATTIK's chart are phenomenal success stories. Ultimately, Scion attracted half a million buyers under the age of 35, ushered over 700,000 buyers into the Toyota family, and elevated automotive marketing to new heights, while selling over U.S. $20 billion-worth of cars. The firm's marketing materials for Swiss Re Tower, acknowledged by a key competitor as being the best marketing suite they had ever seen, helped secure commercial and critical acclaim for 30 St Mary Axe. Icon Aircraft has raised over U.S. $90 million in funding. Within 18 days of its 2009 launch, Free Realms registered its first million users; its base grew to 10 million by 2010. Having raised over U.S. $56 million in funding, OnLive was acquired by Sony in 2015. And the continuing success of Mondelez International (NASDAQ: MDLZ) is beyond question.

Sharing this rocket fuel for your education on the importance of branding is extremely gratifying. If you can put yourself in my shoes, where I was given one of these assignments after another to package and share with the world, I am sure you can imagine my excitement. These exploits led to illustrious career highlights, and many of the most important relationships in my life.

Table 3 Brands by ATTIK

Brand	Year	Scope of Services
Scion (Toyota)	2002–2015	ATTIK named Creative Agency of Record 2 years prior to U.S. brand launch. Responsible for brand identity, strategy, and virtually every facet of U.S. national marketing campaigns through 2015, and for the brand's 2010 launch in Canada.
30 St Mary Axe/ Swiss Re tower	2002–2003	For renowned architect Lord Norman Foster's 40-story skyscraper that dominates London's skyline – known to locals as "the gherkin" – ATTIK developed the brand identity and integrated marketing campaigns for both business-to-business (B2B) and business-to-consumer (B2C) audiences.
Icon Aircraft	2008	To support the launch of ICON Aircraft's A5 consumer sport plane, ATTIK developed the ICON brand identity system (including logo, custom product type face, compositional schemes and color palettes), its website, marketing communications toolset ... and even made design contributions to the A5's exterior and interior (to include the signature red prop).
Free Realms from Sony Online Entertainment	2009	ATTIK created the brand identity system (a complete visual system, including logo art, color palette, typography, and graphic elements) and an integrated campaign for the tween-targeted massive multiplayer online role-playing video game.
OnLive Game Service and OnLive MicroConsole	2009	After seven years of stealth development within the Reardon incubator, OnLive launched at the 2009 Game Developers Conference. ATTIK developed the brand's logo and many other aspects of its visual identity. These included a custom product type face, compositional schemes, color palettes, and the graphics appearing on the MicroConsole and game controller.
Mondelez International	2012	When Kraft Foods decided to separate the "snacks" aspect of its global business representing over U.S. $30 billion in annual revenue, ATTIK was engaged to design the logo and complete visual identity system. The objective was to clearly communicate the brand's personality and higher purpose to a global audience.

74 The Arena

The scenario where ENVOY was ready, willing, and able to connect with Blossom, and the one where ATTIK presented itself as the perfect fit to launch Toyota's new brand to younger drivers in America, have one more poignant angle: The principals of both creative ventures chose me to handle their corporate communications. While these truths are self-evident, I wanted to reinforce the integrity of the information presented here. The ways I set myself – my brand – apart, were enough to get me in the door with these creative industry leaders, who engaged with visionary entrepreneurs and professionals, all of whom became my clients and contemporaries.

I will highlight a few more relevant brand launches quickly. Another client group that elevated every aspect of my existence was Shilo, a creative production company whose inspiring work and brand were well known by the time we engaged in 2008. Like the best of their competitors, Shilo's principals Andre Stringer, Tracy Chandler, Jose Sebastian Gomez, and Danielle Gomez recognized the need to discreetly begin working directly with brands, rather than relying exclusively on advertising agencies for work. This phenomenon was much discussed, as it was both necessary for business success and risky, in that it posed a competitive threat to Shilo's agency clientele. Building on a foundation first established in 2009, drawing on Shilo's own ethos and culture, in 2010 we announced the launch of WMIG as a creative think tank. The vital storytelling elements included a logo, a clear visual identity system (VIS), a website, a powerful original brand film, and a list of clients that already included Amazon.com, Cartoon Network, the San Diego Ad Club, Team Detroit, *The Fader* magazine, and Under Armour.

In 2015, the design and technology event producer FITC decided to mount a new event in Chicago, and they tapped specialized creative agency Leviathan to design the conference's VIS. Well established as a leading FITC speaker, Leviathan's Jason White paired up with his fellow speaker and artist Kim Alpert as creative directors, conceptualizing and locking in the actual conference name, the logo, the poster, the opening titles, collaborating on presenter and sponsor recommendations, and nailing down the Chicago History Museum as its venue. This short documentary shows how successfully it came together.

- FORM 2015 Highlights: https://vimeo.com/146713665

Finally, in 2017, I met the principals of a new venture that was on the verge of being launched, called BIEN. While there were similarities to ATTIK's origin story, this startup stood out for many reasons. Creative Director Hung Le began life in Vietnam; eventually arriving in America to study design and work for top-tier companies across the country, his unique life experiences added some strategic depth. The same is true for Executive Producer Ricardo Roberts. Born in Ecuador, he also grew up and went to school in America, joining Myriad Media in Raleigh, North Carolina, and spending 19 years there as marketing director on his way to becoming a partner.

Based on all our discussions, by the time we were ready to introduce BIEN to the world, you can probably guess what the promotional elements were. These gentlemen had a lovely, simple logo, a VIS, social media channels (Facebook, Instagram, LinkedIn, Twitter), a montage reel, and a story. Their backgrounds and experiences were put in the spotlight, as were their unique perspectives, and their mission of operating a respected international creative shop dedicated to helping the underserved.

Rebrands

This survey of prominent rebrands is sure to drive home your understanding of the elements of branding, as well as how and why these practices work.

Established in 1976, Energias de Portugal (EDP, formerly Electricidade de Portugal) ranks among Europe's major electricity operators, and is one of the world's largest and fastest growing wind energy companies.[9] The entity has published a 40-year study on its brand (http://bit.ly/EDPbrand), fully exploring the story of how its logo evolved over time. As the tale goes, in 2011, the New York City-based creative agency Sagmeister & Walsh was brought onboard to revisit the logo and the visual identity used to represent EDP worldwide. The new system introduced a new monogram with multiple versions of the logo comprised of a circle, a half circle, a square and a triangle ... each of which are layered to create the logos themselves and other icons, to tell the brand's story.

Also using a custom font, the system was introduced in an integrated advertising campaign featuring innovative print, online, television and social media executions, and an extensive catalog of merchandise. My connection to the EDP launch came through the creative studio Brand New School (BNS) responsible for creating the campaign's beautiful, animated content. Just a year earlier, BNS had unveiled a multifaceted "brand expansion" for Cartoon Network, where its approaches emphasized interconnectedness across every promotional asset, as well as the pairing of extremely thoughtful design with animation geared toward generating specific audience responses, including laughter.

In its new system, Cartoon Network embraced its brand visual heritage of a black and white checkerboard by giving it new meaning, and the BNS team executed that idea in fresh, compelling ways, using dimension, color, and movement. Through their diligence, the results also produced a meta-narrative, drawing upon the complete VIS to creatively unify the channel's content. Also featuring a series of 14 animated IDs derived from the letter forms of the newly designed Cartoon Network logo, from the promos to the menus to the bumps to the IDs, each piece told a connected story from a different perspective. According to network executives, the rebrand allowed them to powerfully showcase their full range of exclusive content. By creatively incorporating Cartoon Network's checkerboard design element, BNS reinvigorated the iconic, and introduced fresh excitement throughout the network's diverse range of programming.

2010 was a big year for IGN Entertainment, which by that time was reaching over 44 million unique visitors through its websites, including IGN.com, the premier online destination for videogame content, and the world's top website for reaching men aged 18 to 24. With its headquarters in San Francisco and offices across North America, Europe and Australia, company principals decided it was time to update their 14-year-old brand. Tapping into ATTIK's expertise helping brands maximize communications, particularly in youth markets, the resulting corporate identity for IGN Entertainment better reflected its leadership position within the videogame and entertainment enthusiast markets, while refreshing the consumer-facing IGN.com logo and VIS to extend its appeal and accessibility to continue attracting the exploding audience of gamers.

At ATTIK, the team began by evolving the existing IGN.com icon and letterforms to update their look and feel. Grounded in the iconic "D-pad" used in many game controllers, the site's new logo also featured completely reworked letterforms to give the brand a more contemporary edge. From there, the new IGN Entertainment logo utilized the custom IGN.com letterforms to create a visual link between the two brands, while maintaining a more formal business-to-business feel to heighten the company's credibility with advertisers and partners. Deliverables also included brand guidelines for both IGN Entertainment and IGN.com, business systems for both brands including stationery and presentation materials, numerous promotional elements, and a system and architecture uniting the company's portfolio of media properties. Entering 2010 in top form, IGN successfully launched both brands that January, with updated websites, and through launch events across America.

Several years later, ATTIK took on a rebranding project for Salt Lake City-based Experticity. Founded in 2004, Experticity (renamed ExpertVoice in 2018) serves executives at 750 retail and product brands and the managers of 60,000 retail locations by providing access to its network of over a million active influencers. Led by Creative Director Stu Melvin, ATTIK's team began by creating a platform to help Experticity effectively communicate with its full range of target audiences. The new VIS had two main goals: projecting a memorable, human-centric brand identity reflecting the electric experience of interacting with a passionate expert; and accommodating the brand's need to be effective across all industries.

Retaining the lightning bolt from the previous identity, ATTIK's team incorporated many thoughtful touches in their polished VIS. Among their contributions, they used textures on a warm color palette, handcrafted typography, playful illustrated iconography, and an optimistic style in their photographic elements. After introducing the new website and launching email campaigns, print collateral and videos, the client's creative director highly praised ATTIK's meticulous VIS for giving the brand a world-class identity.

In all these instances, extraordinarily successful companies operating on massive scales reached a point in time when the decision-makers realized that something had to change. Given their objectives and their best strategic thinking, at the core level of what their businesses stood for and how they were perceived, they became convinced that improving their fate demanded a new approach. The difficulty involved in replacing a company's visual identity can be staggering; imagine, for example, the costs EDP faced in rolling out its new identity across its operations. These cases demonstrate how important a logo, and its VIS elements, can be to any business. Use of the IGN identity system spanned over a decade, even following the acquisition of its parent IGN Entertainment by Ziff Davis in 2013. And while Mr. Stockham and his ExpertVoice continue to shine, the branding expertise invested in "Experticity" is still evident.

Finally, I want to share the tales of two smaller businesses where I saw rebrands have considerable impacts. In its first eight years in business, the creative production company Thornberg & Forester (T&F) – built around three extraordinary individuals, none of whom were named Thornberg nor Forester – had done countless things right. The video reel is a staple for creative entities: In 2011, when we teamed up, this company's brilliant version won a Gold Award from Promax, the entertainment marketing association. Continuing to aim high, Co-Founders Elizabeth Kiehner, Scott Matz, and Justin Meredith persisted in focusing on innovative customer support over the next few years. Even while winning new friends and business opportunities, the challenges remained somewhat staggering. In our final collaboration,

I helped T&F generate buzz around a lovely new logo mark, corporate identity, and website, to begin 2014.

While his partners soon left for other ventures, Mr. Matz and Thornberg & Forester live on in New York. His business continues to be successful, which is a credit to his excellent work, including all the sustained efforts to build and manage a compelling brand.

I also love the story from Loretta Jeneski and Michael Degan, partners in a commercial production company launched in Los Angeles in 1995 with a powerful distinction: the directors on their roster all are award-winning documentary filmmakers. Known from its inception as Nonfiction Spots, by the time we began working together in 2006, challenges were arising. More specifically, some of the assignments the team was attracting did not fit under the term "spots," and the company had added an editorial division. That was being addressed in name – with the executives communicating as Nonfiction Spots & Longform, and using a logo consisting of those words in black or white type, set with Courier font – and on the company's website. While my work primarily focused on promoting specific projects, Ms. Jeneski and I returned time and again to the company's name, which seemed to need some finesse we could not devise.

My initial tenure with the firm only ran into 2007, but I was still thrilled in 2008 to see the first news release referring to the venture as "Nonfiction Unlimited (previously Nonfiction Spots)." With a polished new logo, VIS and website, the company was ready to re-introduce itself, and tell its story anew, with complete alignment, nodding to David Baker's wisdom introduced at the top of this chapter. In homage to Scott Goodson, using the name and identity of Nonfiction Unlimited, the group has more distinctly differentiated itself … and is now better positioned to activate and engage internal and external audiences, and the "nonfiction" world where it excels.

Exploration

1. Think about the ideas of "usability" and "elegance" as they apply to a logo and share three examples of logos that you feel meet these descriptions.
2. What does a logo contribute to internal and external perceptions for a brand?
3. Is it truly important to go beyond a logo to develop a VIS, color schemes, and a brand voice? What are the main reasons for your rationale?
4. Provide three examples of brand identities that reflect the target audiences, with a few specific notes on how the connections are made.

5. When it comes to solving branding problems, explain which is more important – analysis or creativity.
6. Think of any website you have seen for a brand and name three things you like most about it.
7. Go on LinkedIn, follow five brands you admire, and spend some time reviewing their company page and their feed. List something new you learn about each company.
8. This chapter provides lessons that apply to consulting firms like mine and yours, as well as big businesses. List three ideas from any company profiled that might help you set yourself apart as a communications consultant.
9. It is your job to help your client company create a brand from scratch: Use the Copy Platform found in chapter 4 to begin framing the assignment.
10. It is your job to help your client company promote a rebrand: Use the Copy Platform to begin framing the assignment.

Notes

1 Goodson, S. (2012, May 27). Why Brand Building Is Important. *Forbes.* http://bit.ly/buildBR.
2 Haden, J. (2011, October 27). The Death of Branding and the Scam of Storytelling. *CBS News.* http://bit.ly/RIPbrand.
3 Sinek, S. (2009, September 1). How Great Leaders Inspire Action. *TED Talks.* http://bit.ly/InspAct.
4 Kagansky, Y. (2020, March 2). Don't Start with Why! | Hacker Noon. *Hacker Noon.* http://bit.ly/dontWHY.
5 Blossom™: The Smart Watering Controller. (2014, November 18). *Kickstarter.* http://kck.st/1yLbJSp.
6 Madans, H. (2016, December 2). Smart Sprinkler Startup in Irvine Bought by Scotts. *Orange County Register.* http://bit.ly/SMgroB.
7 O'Leary, N. (2007, October 26). Dentsu Acquires Attik. *Adweek.* http://adweek.it/2koLT9Q.
8 Coffee, P. (2015, April 30). Dentsu to Absorb Attik after Scion Loss. *AgencySpy.* https://adweek.it/2UX85YH.
9 Wikipedia contributors. (2021, February 15). EDP Group. *Wikipedia.* https://en.wikipedia.org/wiki/Energias_de_Portugal.

8
Business Development

Before beginning to write this subject matter, I was already well familiar with at least 20 books dedicated to the subject of sales. In comparison to those authors, my qualifications as an expert on sales/business development are limited. Still, when it comes to operating a communications consultancy – and providing high-level support to other sophisticated companies where the quality of their products and services are among the world's best – my track record has illuminated many tried-and-true insights into attracting and closing new business.

According to science, I am likely to be 50% more successful in solving a puzzle if I use "interrogative self-talk," versus just telling myself I will succeed.[1] I learned this from Daniel Pink's book *To Sell is Human*, and he drove his point home by providing a great example of this type of approach to life: He used Bob the Builder, and his often-heard refrain, asking if we can fix something, then answering affirmatively and emphatically. Our objective here is to illuminate the realm of business development, and to provide some strategies for the successful handling of sales matters. Am I capable of teaching you important lessons about business development? Absolutely.

What Sales Means to Me

Looking back, my plans for life after high school graduation were short-sighted. Every next-level aspiration hinged on earning a U.S. Air Force scholarship. Failing that, the plan became finding a job and paying my way through college. By then, my paid experience included working in a department store, phone soliciting, and a sort of dream job working at hotel swimming pools in Orlando, where I was unofficially an activity director, and officially a Panama Jack sunscreen salesman. That latter job through Resort Pool Management (RPM) employed many outgoing young people, and some were remarkably successful. I was bottom rung, which was reflected

DOI: 10.4324/9781003177951-8

in my U.S. $25 per day rate. In my mind, it came down to this: I was less interested in pressuring people to buy sunscreen than in making new friends and chilling out.

Seeking to improve my professional situation, I answered ads for sales positions promising hundreds of dollars per day, and soon found myself in one "cattle call" situation after another. To my surprise (at first), I always got the job. Without fail, they all were purely commission-based. I was hired to sell phone book ads, audiotape club memberships, vacuum cleaners ... and eventually, an annuity life insurance policy for ITT Life. ITT was a classic boiler room scenario right out of a movie. Unlike those other sales opportunities, the traits of others I saw succeeding in the ITT Life office hooked me and my determination. I went through intensive sales training to learn the ropes of prospecting, qualifying, presenting, and closing, then was sent out "into the field." There, the goal was to be able to visit a home – usually by cold-calling (in other words, we just knocked on doors) – and sell an insurance policy on-the-spot; return visits were forbidden. We worked six days a week, starting at 9 a.m. and ending our days after 8 p.m.

I had taken this job, and earned my license to sell insurance, to make lots of money. After about five months, flat broke, I gave up on the experiment, enlisted to enter the Air Force a few months later, and began working several different jobs for hourly wages. My first paycheck from the Air Force allowed me to settle my debts, and in the fall of 1985 – 16 months after high school graduation – with help from the G.I. Bill, I enrolled at the University of Central Florida.

I previously shared my story about working at TTG, starting The Darnell Works Agency upon my departure, and then leaving Los Angeles for North Carolina. Sales in LA had been one thing, when I was able to network and field opportunities like those that came about from the referrals of Lisa Cleff and others. In Boone, I became even more dependent on referrals, and my primary focus for generating them was giving my roster clients excellent service so they would stick with me, and so they would endorse and recommend me. In 2012, completely by surprise, I learned about a more scientific approach to sales.

In January of that year, I joined 100 other creative-industry entrepreneurs in Nashville at the ReCourses New Business Summit (NBS), hosted by David C. Baker and Blair Enns. The subtitle for the event was, "Using Your Positioning for More Reward, Impact, Control, and Fun." To set my personal stage in more detail, revenue for DWA in 2011 was down 15% compared with the previous year, and even my most reliable clients were starting to get a little shaky. Still, I was sticking with my plan of providing excellent service to all those on retainer, while systematically beginning to better track and engage with anyone who contacted me to discuss work. For the first time ever, my 2011 year-end holiday greetings sent to clients contained a special message, informing them I would be taking a month off the following summer, to explore Yellowstone and some of America's other National Parks with my family. In other words, despite facing some serious concerns in my business, I also knew that our kids were growing up fast, and that the opportunity to forge a bold, adventurous travel experience with them could easily slip away. One might call this approach a leap of faith.

Here is a more detailed assessment of the main sales tactics I was using at that time.

- Retainer Engagements based on Hourly Rate: Generally, my retainer clients started at U.S. $3,000 per month, and our agreement was based on the deal letter clarifying my hourly rate and other terms. Paid at the beginning of each month, I aimed to provide services based on my allotted hours. This represents the "don't forget to ask for the check" tactic I learned selling life insurance for ITT Life, and the sales and closing strategies I honed there and at TTG, where the industry standard allowed the firm to get paid in advance.
- Referrals and Inbound Inquiries: I had recently started methodically cataloging the inquiries I received (95% by email, the rest by phone). Previously I would politely tell prospects that my roster was full and refer them to others, but at this point – even if the roster was full – I began making more of an effort to seize the day to get to know prospects. After speaking together, those individuals were added to a list, I sent them a Thanksgiving and/or holiday message, and I alerted my top pick(s) when I had a client opening.
- Main Tools: Business-to-business focused website including sales kit elements and case studies … and consistent use of key social media channels: LinkedIn and Twitter.
- Main Marketing Tactics: For companies I sought to work with, I followed a 1–2–3 "interview, bid, contract" approach. I also fielded inquiries and strategically managed communications to include prospects. By then, I was publishing an article per week on my blog and cross-promoting it on Twitter.
- Key Marketing Messages: Expertise, Confidence, and Scarcity. Through my activities, blog posts, and social feeds, I made a lot of effort to *demonstrate* my expertise. My positioning consistently conveyed my dedication to a "short list of phenomenally talented companies," which exuded confidence – and proved to be attractive.

Now, imagine being in the room with all those entrepreneurs in Nashville in 2012, when Mr. Baker asked us to tell him what the word "sales" meant to us. By now, you have gained many insights into the map my mind illuminated. A few people offered familiar answers along the lines of picking up the phone, pounding the pavement, knocking on doors, asking for checks. The conference leader then explained that if we followed their prescribed methodologies, sales would become saying yes or no to whoever calls.

Let's fast forward two years from that moment. Much of the gospel shared at NBS 2012 had infiltrated my business, and thanks to the mentorship of conference alumni G. Scott Shaw of Everclear Marketing, I launched a greatly improved website in 2013. As one measure of its success, referrals went up 18% that year, and climbed another 16% in 2014. And I will never forget one call I had in 2014, which went something like this. "I see on your website that your roster is full, that you don't handle one-off projects, and your minimum retainer is U.S. $3,000 per month. But we have a one-off project we were hoping you'd be interested in." My response was, thank you very much, but no. Hanging up, as I added another name to my prospect list, I realized that sales for my business had evolved to the exact place Mr. Baker had promised.

The Importance of Sales in Marketing

Quickly, I want to backtrack a bit more to illuminate the importance of the sales function within marketing, from my point of view. In the late 80s, I can still recall sitting in class at UCF when the manager of an Orlando radio station was brought in to speak with us. Hearing how the most common path for a general manager was for them to <u>come from sales</u> added to my knowledge of publishers having to be adept in the sales profession. Since then, the absolute dependence of business success on selling has become abundantly clear.

In my role as a press release writer for Century III at Universal Studios Florida (C3), my boss was the head of sales and marketing, and her orchestration of a multifaceted marketing plan – leveraging a potent combination of advertising expenditures, association memberships, sponsorships, editorial-focused PR efforts and tightly managed sales activities – drove the ambitious venture to amazing heights. Her account executives comprising her sales force were the primary sources for the project-based stories we generated, each of which served the marketing objectives of the company, leading to wider recognition and more sales. In other words, those individuals responsible for converting leads into customers provided the essential ingredients for virtually all marketing efforts, providing the vital evidence of C3's value to its customers and demonstrating the successful fulfillment of its promises as a brand.

Several years later, my boss at Crest National in Hollywood brought me into a similar operation. Also the head of sales and marketing for an ambitious venture, where he managed a team mirroring C3's, John Walker designed and executed his own multifaceted marketing plan, driving Crest to new heights as Hollywood's one-stop film, video, and optical media services company. Once again, my role was virtually identical: Finding the best-case studies for new projects and bringing them to greater attention through PR and marketing efforts. Each of those case studies existed due to a sale.

When I landed as the director of marketing for The Spark Factory, company principal Tim Street was looking to me to handle every role under the marketing umbrella. Suddenly, I had a very real appreciation for all the situations where I had not needed to generate sales myself. Despite being more attracted to marketing efforts, like developing sponsorships and placing news stories, I had to commit to targeting prospects and prompting them along the sales funnel toward purchase. From my days at RPM to those at ITT Life and all these other companies, the steps of the sales process remained consistent: prospecting, qualifying, presenting, and closing.

My next career move led me back to the communications consultant position, where I could largely rely on others in the marketing department to manage new business. Still, as an account executive at TTG, I was tasked with landing new accounts. Among my other duties were organizing and updating both custom press kits and sales kits that we used to demonstrate our experience and expertise, all of which took digital form, could be posted and shared online, and were key components in closing new business. Worth noting at TTG, due to the reputation of the company and its principal Michael Terpin, we experienced a steady stream of inbound referrals.

Back on my own with The Darnell Works Agency (DWA) in 2000, my own sales kit proved to be an especially important tool in closing new accounts, and I learned that clients wanted to see case studies documenting how I had impacted my clients' successes. These elements came together on my website and in my proposal materials, to facilitate sales efforts for DWA.

In summary, ultimately, transacting business always begins with closing a sale. As the seller, I must be able to demonstrate the value of what I am selling, and convince my client it is worth the cost. If clients or buyers are not coming to me, I must either draw them in or go find them.

In a 2018 Marketing Week Article, a representative from holiday group TUI delineates marketing and sales jobs by referring to the first group's mission as attracting targets, so that they can be converted by sales.[2] Fulfilling those complementary but distinct objectives requires unique approaches, which are most effective when coordinated closely.

Adapting to Pull/Inbound/Permission/Content Marketing

By and large, the Internet has revolutionized the way the world does business, and based on its existence, other innovations are now shifting the related buyer-seller relationship parameters in new ways. For companies that cannot afford to blast massive audiences with TV, radio or online ads, there are smarter ways to get messages out; in fact, there are even smarter messages.

In the forward to Jay Baer's 2013 book "Youtility," entrepreneur and sales expert Marcus Sheridan shares fascinating details about the marketing tactics used by his U.S.-based company, River Pools and Spas. Contrasting his approach to advertising in 2007's vibrant economy when selling pools was a breeze (investing six percent of his U.S. $4 million gross proceeds), he admits to cutting his ad spend below one percent in 2011's sagging economy, while boosting sales to U.S. $4.5 million. How was this miraculous feat accomplished?

By Mr. Sheridan's account, it began with positioning. Instead of being swimming pool builders, they began describing themselves and acting as teachers on the subject of swimming pools, who also happen to build them.[3] To the best of my understanding, Mr. Sheridan's tale of becoming a *Youtility* instead of just a swimming pool company is another way of saying that they adopted a marketing approach that can be described as content, permission, inbound and/or pull marketing.

At NBS in 2012, Mark O'Brien was one of the guest speakers we met on a day that began with Blair Enns telling us this how, for most of us, the gap between marketing and sales was shrinking. Mr. O'Brien has also written a book, entitled *A Website That Works*, which carries an endorsement from Mr. Enns on its jacket. Acknowledging O'Brien's keen understanding of the immense value of agency websites for sales and marketing, he recommends the book as a key to improving business development.

My notes from Mr. O'Brien's presentation confirm his enlightened point of view. After addressing how the web has changed the relationship between sales and marketing, he then explained that creative agencies can either adapt to "pull marketing" and succeed, or stick with "push marketing" strategies and perish. Push (or outbound, or interruption) marketing is represented by the large-scale advertising efforts of brands like Coca Cola, which often are interrupting you during some experience you are having where you probably are not about to buy a soft drink. The alternative approach is pull marketing, where Coca Cola and the rest of us draw buyers to us (often, our websites or our apps), and engage with them more directly.

Through the example provided by Mr. Sheridan explaining the shift from being a swimming pool builder to being expert teachers on the subject of swimming pools, I am sure you can guess the basic differences between how his company's website looked in 2007 versus how it looked in 2011 ... and how the subject matter of its ad campaigns from those two different eras would vary.

Régis Lemmens is a consultant, author, and teacher on the topic of sales and sales management who has co-authored articles and books examining the future of sales, including *From Selling to Co-Creating*. In a 2014 TED Talk, he described how the adoption of pull marketing strategies is creating value for buyers that, in the best cases, makes them willing to pay.[4] Whereas past sales approaches have traditionally proceeded from targeting to persuading, he sees that second step shifting to "co-creating," where needs are addressed with the benefits of a product or service. Therefore, the new version of sales is to partner, collaborate, and deliver.

These insights support the case for sales and marketing generally getting closer together, and Mr. Ellis of TUI confirms how that phenomenon frames his company's marketing approach. Calling it "sales through service," TUI's aim as an organization is to maximize its sales efforts by focusing on providing extraordinary service. That may ring a bell for you, based on hearing how I have focused my marketing efforts at DWA.

Still, in 2012, when asked what sales meant to me, I did not immediately think of waiting for the phone to ring so I could say yes or no. So, what changed to make my website – and my marketing efforts – more effective following the consulting efforts of Mr. Shaw, who had fully grasped the teachings of Mr. Baker, Mr. Enns, and Mr. O'Brien?

1. Positioning
Remember that the subtitle for the 2012 New Business Summit was "Using Your Positioning for More Reward, Impact, Control, and Fun." At the summit, my positioning was strengthened, and I learned a ton about the rationale for distilling and communicating my expertise, and using that to pursue new business strategically.

2. Writing
Mr. O'Brien is adamant about the need to consistently write new material demonstrating one's expertise, and adding that to one's website. He suggests

2,000 words per month. I was coming close to that already; however, Mr. Shaw's advice reminded me to be bolder and more specific in setting myself apart through my website's writing. To that end, I focused on building and regularly updating two new sections, extolling client news and agency results.

3. Explaining Terms of Doing Business
   There are many invaluable aspects of the business development framework that came to light across the NBS event. Among those, Mr. Enns talked us through the establishment of a basic threshold engagement prospects must meet to begin doing business together.[5] Today, mine begins with potential clients committing to U.S. $3,500 per month for at least a few months. Thanks to the expert counsel I received, this information first appeared on my website in 2013, and since then, this and other aspects of working with me have become regular talking points discussed with all potential new clients.

While there is much more to learn about positioning and content marketing, this introduction to business development is sure to help you understand how and why client relationships are changing. With the existence of a worldwide web of information, and the ability for individuals to access it with ease while also leveraging the insights and recommendations of others – including machines driven by artificial intelligence – most people can find potential sources to fulfill their needs. When our strategic communications efforts can attract them to our threshold and qualify our products/services as being viable and valuable, if the selling organization feels the customer is a good fit, the close is seamlessly transitioning buyers into customer service.

Exploration

1. Think of a difficult situation you are facing where you can use "interrogative self-talk" to mentally prepare yourself ... then use it and describe the results.
2. *Prospecting* remains an important initial step in marketing because it allows us to skew our communications efforts to the right people. Imagine owning a pool installation company – and list ten types of individuals you think might be worth targeting. What are the top three groups, and why?
3. Think about how qualifying works for a communications consultancy, and list three situations in which you would choose not to work with a company that is ready to write you a check.
4. Why is it important for you to be able to communicate your expertise early into your relationships with your business prospects?

5. Prepare three case studies you can use in your work that will help you communicate how you have impacted the success of others, and help you attract potential clients.
6. Research sales kits – track down at least three from other consultants or businesses and explain how each kit distinguishes an important trait for its subject company.
7. Research press kits – track down at least three from other consultants or businesses and explain how each kit distinguishes an important trait for its subject company.
8. Many of today's top sales experts emphasize the importance not just of problem-solving, but of solving the right problem. What is the difference, do you feel the distinction is important, and if so, why?
9. What does "sales" mean to you? Share your brief or extended thoughts.
10. How can scarcity heighten demand for a product or service? Provide three examples.

Notes

1 Pink, D.H. (2012). *To Sell Is Human* [Hardcover]. Penguin Random House USA.
2 Rogers, C. (2018, March 28). Why There Is 'No Excuse for Misalignment' Between Marketing and Sales. *MarketingWeek*. http://bit.ly/MSalign.
3 Baer, J. (2013). *Youtility: Why Smart Marketing Is about Help Not Hype*. Portfolio.
4 TEDx Talks. (2014, June 18). Sales 2020: Regis Lemmens at TEDxLiege [Video]. *YouTube*. https://youtu.be/cYV9irrztIc.
5 Enns, B. (2021, February 16). Should You Publish Pricing on Your Website? *Win Without Pitching*. http://bit.ly/mloe18.

9
Customer Service

In the same ways that successful businesses demand an emphasis on sales to facilitate income, it is also well understood that there must be stewards of customer service actively working to ensure buyers are having positive experiences. Surprisingly, extraordinarily good service is rare ... so it is easy to think that customer service functions – and the desired CX – must not be especially important. Nothing could be further from the truth.

Operating The Darnell Works Agency, I have had to emphasize sterling customer service for my clients, to compensate for not living in one of the major markets where most of them operate. Here is a measure of my success turning that potential negative into a positive: My average client engagement across 44 different client companies exceeds 33 months. In a world where positive CX is not the norm, I want to shine a light on the mission-critical benefits of making them the priority.

Leading CX research, consulting, and training firm Qualtrics XM Institute (QXMI) is widely known for its annual study rating customer interactions according to customers' perceptions of success, effort, and emotion. For several years, these words introduced the report: "To improve customer experience, companies need to master four competencies: Purposeful Leadership, Compelling Brand Values, Employee Engagement, and Customer Connectedness."[1] Let's use that framework to illuminate the foundation created by CX success.

Leaders' Emphasis on CX

When I started handling PR accounts for TTG in Los Angeles, one of the management notes that came down from the company's leaders told us we should make contact on each of our accounts daily. I have found a lot of wisdom in that imperative: People are likely to feel they are a priority when they

DOI: 10.4324/9781003177951-9

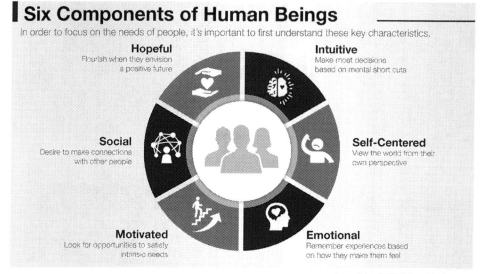

Figure 3 Six Components of Human Beings.[2]

hear from you every day. This is equally true, as I have found: Diligence and effort are required to ensure that daily contact is meaningful and productive.

When this type of focus is applied to making daily progress in serving a company's main objectives, there is value. Further, you also stand to become extremely familiar as a co-worker, team-member, key contributor … and even as a friend, potentially.

J.D. Power produces an annual study focused specifically on the automotive service industry. Company VP Chris Sutton emphasized several key points when introducing the 2018 edition.[3] Citing the latest research, he pointed out how all success for a dealer's reputation relies on satisfied customers, who are likely to return, and pass along recommendations. Dealers who are unable to make customers happy, he advised, will probably lose them to competitors who can.

This is exactly the type of phenomenon I was counting on leveraging after my wife suggested leaving L.A. My first reaction was, finding the right kind of clients in Boone, North Carolina, seemed unlikely. After a few days, that became, maybe I can convince my clients to stick with me. My experience at TTG also taught me that even adeptly managed PR firms that regularly attract new referrals are not necessarily focused on retaining their clients; based on what I had observed, much of the emphasis was on new accounts.

So, for me, because of life choices and desires, I was willing to take a chance on prioritizing customer service in the hope it would pay off in the ways Mr. Sutton suggested.

Not only did I commit to doing excellent work for the small number of companies on my roster, knowing how important they were to me and all aspects of my life, I had to use every tool at my disposal to make myself invaluable and attractive to them. John Coleman is the co-author of the book *Passion & Purpose: Stories from the Best and Brightest Young Business Leaders*. He contributed a thoughtful article to the *Harvard Business Review* discussing the importance of purpose.[4] Here is my takeaway: Positive work relationships make all jobs more fulfilling ... and even mundane work becomes meaningful alongside people we care about and connect with.

I am deeply proud to know that one in seven of the companies DWA has engaged with – to include several currently on my roster – have stuck with me for over four years. The commitment to customer service and extraordinary CX is not guaranteed to produce lifelong business relationships, but this formula is proven to help the best relationships go surprisingly far.

Brand Values that Compel

It is one thing to say I want to make myself indispensable to my clients, but how does that translate into the right types of daily activities, week after week, month after month? When I am beginning a new relationship, I must make the case with every new client that I am here to perform for them, and if I fail to meet their expectations, I want them to be free to seek out a better fit. Matching the key customer perceptions QXMI uses to evaluate CX, I have learned to communicate DWA's high aims for success, effort, and emotional connections with my clients from the beginning. In other words, I see the first steps of telling and showing them I care – and demonstrating that I will be working hard to please them – as being vital. When you are the client, hearing that your service provider is deeply committed to extraordinary service is powerful medicine.

Naturally, from there, the standing requirement is to measure up, and there are many processes, tools, and practices I use to stay focused and to keep my efforts on track. Many client engagements begin in a similar place ... where a company realizes it has communications needs. For someone known to have expertise in media relations, this need is usually a story that the management wants told, ideally involving the media. As often as not, management may see that objective as an isolated situation – a project. For any organization that has not actively engaged with a communications consultant over an extended time, the commitment to getting a story out to the world seems to be impulsive, and not something they want to take on regularly. When I have an interest in a group that presents me with a project opportunity, I usually seize the moment to share my own compelling brand values with them – pointing out the virtues of adding professional communications expertise to their core capabilities and committing to maximizing them over time. There are many benefits I can illuminate relatively quickly … including pointing out how the results of media engagement usually increase exponentially when pursued diligently over time. By and large, the rest of my "close" aims to educate them on how a sustained PR program is an essential tool for shaping and demonstrating a company's leadership, setting the company apart in its marketplace … and engaging and honoring its human resources and its customers.

When the terms are fair and easy to accept, and when I present myself as diligent, responsive, proven, respectful, professional, and dedicated, the brand values I put forward translate into a step the client must be willing to take to begin defining – and fulfilling – their larger corporate vision. Sometimes they are still not ready to take that step; even then, I am proud to help them better understand the reasons why an ongoing commitment to PR may be in their long-term best interest.

In the same way this applies to me, your own commitment to learning the philosophies, skills, and processes laid out in this curriculum can position you as the solution to a company's commitment to sustainable, long-term success, which prioritizes extraordinary customer service and CX.

I will have more details to share with you on processes, helping you to understand deep-level strategic plans like communications audits and marketing plans, which then feed into vital initiatives ranging from designing and executing integrated marketing campaigns to strategically handling social media posts. For now, consider the following anecdotes reflecting proven insights of some other well-established leaders.

In his teachings, Blair Enns lays out the four main phases of client engagement like so: 1 diagnose the problem; 2 prescribe a strategy or solution; 3 implement the strategy; 4 ongoing re-implementation.[5] Further, he classifies the first two phases as "thinking," and the last two as "doing," then advises his students to emphasize the thinking parts in their work. For me, this wisdom is applied as a constant reminder to be innovative in setting the agenda for my client-directed activities, and in carrying out each day's task work.

In Mr. Enns' article referenced above, the importance of a diagnosis is heavily emphasized. The first step to addressing a problem is making a hypothesis, which is either proven or disproven by testing. As a consultant, finding the right paths to validating hypotheses – to then be able to accurately diagnose and treat (or to properly "serve" in the delivery of customer service) – is where art and diplomacy meets science and diligence.

Consider the science of problem finding, which has been studied exhaustively by psychologists Jacob Getzels and Mihaly Csikszentmihalyi. An insight from their findings appears in a *Science* magazine article from Linda Austin, M.D.[6] To skilled problem finders, she attributes the quality of being able to examine quandaries – even those that have stood for ages – comprehend them in new ways, and devise completely original solutions.

To be an invaluable communications consultant capable of contributing impactful solutions to clients on an ongoing basis, one must commit to innovative problem-finding, and become a dedicated, responsive shaper of strategic subject matter and intelligent communications tactics. By embracing this mindset and its attendant skill sets and methodologies with a dedication to service and ongoing education, your willingness, and your abilities to serve will make you highly compelling.

Engaging Human Resources

In chapter 5, a 2014 survey is cited where 15,000 millennial college students specify "cultural fit" as their top criterion for companies they want to work for. The same section conveys more insights from Elise Mitchell, where she attributes her former company's high retention rate to its family-like culture. I have seen and heard similar stories from many companies I have worked with, leading me to appreciate the common ingredients in workplaces where employees enjoy their work and exhibit loyalty.

Happily, many of the companies I have worked with the longest consistently foster high job satisfaction and retention among their star employees. Surely, my efforts surfacing insights of these companies' – and their employees' – actual work in service of their actual clients, and helping to make those stories visible to the public, have been impactful. In fact, much of my diligence on behalf of my clients results in greater recognition for their employees, which increases their job satisfaction. As another angle into this phenomenon, many of my client engagements have started with this problem: A key employee complains to management that the company and its work deserve more recognition. Whether by management understanding the company has stories to tell the world, or the insistence of a VIP employee or outsider, this is the type of spark that often leads my phone to ring. From there, relatively quickly, we are discussing how any scenario where a company or employee hopes to gain recognition requires an outstanding CX rating.

Whether the emphasis is on employee job satisfaction or positive CX, the company truly focusing on being successful is sure to find common ground connecting both initiatives. A savvy communications consultant is bound to uncover company strengths and weaknesses, opportunities, and threats, in sustained efforts assessing its clients' human resources.

Connecting to Customers

When we talk about emphasizing customers, we are in the sweet spot for discussions of corporate communications strategy. If there are no customers, there is no business. Honoring those who have chosen to do business, who are experiencing positive CX, is not only the intelligent means for keeping them positively engaged, but also the shrewd marketing approach to attracting new customers.

The proverb "nothing succeeds like success" conveys the time-honored logic here. When a business can demonstrate even one bout of customer success, it has an engaging example to share with others proving its value. There is more to the story, of course; consumers demand high ratings across numerous transactions, and they also want to be able to see if there have been bad experiences that provide further insights into the company they are considering doing business with.

Across all a company's public touchpoints, the communications jobs related to customer service can focus on elements spanning from the physical (building locations, signage, offices, uniforms, ballcaps) to the digital (website, social media channels, apps). It is no secret: Anywhere extraordinarily positive CX is happening, bringing them to wider attention is generally rewarded. Indeed, most of my client engagements begin with the delivery of a monumental, client-driven project. In the chapter discussing Objectives, you will recall that OpenText's research builds up Customer Engagement as the absolute most important business objective. What they proclaim as the business of the future is one that is dedicated to the Continuous Connected Customer Journey. We also have time-honored wisdom from both Mahatma Gandhi and Martin Luther King, Jr., ranking service to others among life's highest callings.

Every example and lesson provided in this chapter validates that wisdom. In my own journey, I have found my value in attending to the needs of my clients. The hallmark case studies tend to focus on those companies I travel with over long spans of time, and yet, even for companies where we have started and ended in a matter of weeks, I am proud of the impact I made, the education gained, and whatever understanding I was able to help manifest. Sometimes, a company's management wants to be able to tell its heroic story of positive customer experiences ... and yet, maybe the project did not turn out as planned, possibly because a key player dropped out along the way. It is difficult – at times, impossible – to successfully navigate the power structure among client companies, and this reality is a barrier to communications for my clients, and my clients' clients. Other impediments to customer service, and to communications activities that might put them in the spotlight, include the solidity of any company's management approaches, and how those empower or constrain employees. Fittingly, when money is tight, it is hard to expect the customer service to be top-notch.

For the communications consultant, the ability to assess a potential client's CX track record is yet another solid prescription for understanding its pedigree, and its prospects for future success. Even if the history is scarred, a real commitment to customer service is a proven, exceptional talking point ... especially when the customers truly are happy.

Exploration

1. Name two examples of a "service" situation you have encountered where you were left feeling unimportant. List something the vendor could have done to improve your satisfaction.
2. Name two examples of a "service" situation you have encountered where you told someone about your positive experience. What were the keys to creating the CX, from your perspective?
3. List five relationship benefits that are made possible by a commitment to daily contact.
4. DWA clients regularly hear that I am very proud to be part of their team. What are the main benefits of such words in fostering positive CX?
5. For a real or imaginary company seeking to bolster public perceptions of its strengths as a business, provide three examples of stories it might tell that you would expect to be effective.
6. For the scenario described in your answer to question five, now imagine that the company has consistently been rated poorly in customer service. Does that change your story examples? If so, how?
7. One classic example of "problem finding" innovation is a building with a slow elevator, where the ingenious solution is to install mirrors to give people something else to focus on. Given a problem of a company

needing to build its positive reputation, list three ideas that are equally imaginative.
8. Whereas many clients who might contract with a communications consultant begin by thinking "project basis," there are obvious reasons why the consultant would want them to think longer term (like, fewer sales demands for the consultant). Prepare an "elevator speech" to explain why committing longer term may make more sense for any business; this is bound to serve your business well.
9. You have interest from a company you can surmise has a great reputation: List five potential benefits of working with this company, identify the one you feel best about, and explain your choice.
10. You have interest from a company you can surmise has a spotty reputation: List five potential benefits of working with this company, identify the one you feel best about, and explain your choice.

Notes

1 Temkin, B. (2016, March 8). Report: 2016 Temkin Experience Ratings. *Customer Experience Matters®*. http://bit.ly/16TExpR.
2 Temkin, B. (2020, September 29). The Six Key Traits of Human Beings (Blog). *XM Institute*. http://bit.ly/HActsVid.
3 2018 U.S. Customer Service Index Study. (2018, March 15). *J.D. Power*. http://bit.ly/JDP18csi.
4 Coleman, J. (2017, December 29). To Find Meaning in Your Work, Change How You Think about It. *Harvard Business Review*. http://bit.ly/WorkThnk.
5 Enns, B. (2018, March 16). First, Do No Harm. *Win Without Pitching*. http://bit.ly/wwpnoharm.
6 Austin, L. (2009, February 20). Perspective: Problem Finding and the Multidisciplinary Mind. *AAAS/Science*. http://bit.ly/probfind.

10
Integrated Marketing in Action

As we focus-in on the role of the communications consultant, which most often will be applied under the banner of public relations (PR) activities, it is important to have a solid understanding of all facets of The Promotional Mix. Individually and in concert, this group of activities represents a company's means for attracting and engaging with customers and communicating its values. Representing numerous disciplines, individuals, and corporate investments, oftentimes, the PR field is where it all comes together and unites to serve the overall mission.

Never forget the Continuous Connected Customer Journey, the importance of fostering positive Customer Experiences (CX), and all the benefits that come from a daily commitment to the customers of any business. Delivering strategic brand messages effectively has always required diligence and even nuance to be effective; these days, businesses are pushing the limits of machine learning and automation to maximize their connections and CX. While all of that can be intimidating, many bright business executives emphasize this: Very often, everything comes down to storytelling, which is a primary function of PR.

In their authoritative book *Advertising and Promotion: An Integrated Marketing Communications Perspective*, George and Michael Belch present an incredibly detailed chapter specifically about integrated marketing.[1] Here, we will survey this terrain by dividing up The Promo Mix into five categories: advertising; sales promotion; personal selling; direct and digital marketing; and PR. By exploring each of these elements in the context of a handful of campaigns, the roles and responsibilities of communications consultants become more evident.

In our work, the key skill set involves Account Management, Customer Service, Planning, Writing, Media Relations, Measurement, and Reporting.

DOI: 10.4324/9781003177951-10

Primarily, we function as Analyst and Historian, Strategist and Chief Communications Officer (CCO), Patron of Sales, Patron of Customer Service, Relationship Developer, Storyteller, and/or Marketing Maven. In the other realms where The Promotional Mix comes to life, there are people whose roles and responsibilities overlap with these functions. For example, advertising account directors must also be mindful of all this territory, to ensure strategies and tactics align to address campaign objectives. Behind all the plans and actions, there are client marketers: the CEO, the chief marketing officer, and their team members. If every aspect of a plan is not tightly integrated, that is a reflection on them, their organization, leadership, and brand.

GEICO

One company that consistently uses integrated marketing is the U.S.-based Government Employees Insurance Company (GEICO). In every medium (TV, radio, online, and offline), the company's commercials are consistently hilarious, and ubiquitous, fully covering the advertising element. Sales promotions are tied to the ads, and draw from other categories of the mix, to incentivize target audiences to save money, one of the brand's core values and objectives. With such an active, integrated marketing machine, much of the personal selling has to do with answering the phone, but also, for agents, arranging and taking personal meetings to close prospects as new customers. Direct and digital marketing efforts consist of mailings, coupons, online banners, and takeovers. To see its PR campaign at work, uniting all these activities to impact positive CX in the context of the continuous connected customer journey, visit http://twitter.com/GEICO. That is integrated marketing in action.

"Roseanne"

On May 29, 2018, the "hit" revival version of this television show was abruptly put to rest by ABC, in response to some controversial tweets from its star, Roseanne Barr, earlier that day. While the story arc has carried forward, this meteoric turn of events makes a fascinating case study for assessing The Promotional Mix at work, while demonstrating the volatility introduced by social media and continuously connected customer journeys.

Let's begin in May 2017, at the Upfronts, ABC's annual sales conference for buyers of TV advertising. Like its competitive TV networks CBS and NBC, the Alphabet Network has been convening buyers to promote its best shows in New York City for decades. For the 2017 edition at Lincoln Center, the Disney-owned network re-introduced the program's Conner family and friends, in announcing the 2018 return of "Roseanne" to the airwaves after a 20-year hiatus. According to media reports, that publicity stunt staged for buyers of TV advertising did not go over so well, and lowered some expectations for the revival.[2]

By early 2018, however, the marketing machinery was in full swing, expanding the focus from buyers of TV advertising to TV viewers in major markets. Following its sales promotions for media buyers and building upon the personal sales efforts of those at the network responsible for selling out their commercial inventory, consumer advertising elements began appearing at the highest levels. At large-scale consumer and industry gatherings like SXSW, fans could visit and interact with the show's most famous sets. In major cities across the country, the iconic Conner family couch – complete with knitted afghan – was introduced at bus stops and in subway trains. The fact that this build-up was so well documented in the media reflects the full-strength PR effort that complemented all other campaign facets, ensuring that journalists and reporters understood all the activities afoot, and most of all, when and where Roseanne would return to the airwaves on March 27.

At a time when subscription-based streaming media platforms and other digital means for accessing original content were eclipsing the reach of TV's advertising-driven business model, the return of "Roseanne" introduced a vastly different talking point. In total, more than 18 million people tuned into the premiere broadcast, winning the night's ratings battle by a landslide. A few days later, ABC announced it would produce another season. If the PR teams were not already slammed, every aspect of the program's – and the network's – storytelling now demanded more attention. Naturally, the show's new iteration brought renewed interest to the original series. ABC's marketing team seized the opportunities around the new broadcasts and online, including with its ABC app, where viewers can access network shows at home or on-the-go using smartphones, tablets, computers, and over-the-top services like Amazon Prime Video, Hulu, and Netflix. The billions of new CX happening around "Roseanne" reached a peak in late May, after broadcasting the entire new season 10, as the network and everyone behind the show invited viewers to binge "Roseanne" over the Memorial Day weekend, and to ready themselves for season 11. Riding high atop the show's monumentally successful return, ABC's marketers enjoyed premier status at their 2018 Upfronts; for the first time in 24 years, they owned America's top-rated TV series.[3]

But of course, you already know where this winds up. Returning to our earliest discussions about reputation management, personal brands, and objectives ... when you build everything around Roseanne Barr, her beliefs and values are part of your foundation. Most often, social media channels are managed as part of PR promotions, for very good reasons: For better or worse, tweets and Instagram posts now stand for quotes in news coverage. That certainly was true for the 2018 story of "Roseanne," where Ms. Barr's tweets – grossly out-of-alignment with ABC's marketing platform – promptly drove Disney's entire ABC juggernaut to a complete U-turn… leading to the network distributing a one-sentence statement from ABC Entertainment's president canceling the show.

Across every facet of The Promotional Mix spectrum, every category of activity reached meteoric heights for "Roseanne," and clearly, the entire slate was tightly integrated. The unbridled lovefest mounted by one of America's most powerful media networks turned into full-scale abandonment by everyone involved over the course of one American Memorial Day. As an integrated team, every marketer behind the show had no choice but to start explaining what would come in the aftermath, striving to fortify positive CX and to provide value to business partners who had engaged in every way possible – including financially – around a property that died overnight. Still, from the bottom to the top of the organization, ABC presented itself as a well-managed force that was able to pivot, when necessary, to honor its core values and serve its most cherished objectives, and its customers.

ATTIK and Scion

My only role in the sensational "Roseanne" rollercoaster was as a curious onlooker, but there are many integrated marketing campaigns I have been actively involved with over the years. Still, the experiences I gained representing global creative agency ATTIK during its tenure as creative agency of record for Toyota's youth-targeted Scion brand form the foundation of my education in large-scale brand communications. Thanks to Scion's remarkable leaders, as part of a phenomenal agency team, I had the opportunity to support, amplify, and learn from hallmark brand values like these: bold, innovative thinking; magnificently authentic marketing; and customer service better described as customer reverence.

ATTIK – which became a bona fide agency on July 15, 2002, the day Scion awarded the firm creative duties for its U.S. launch – earned its place in maverick fashion, by enshrining the importance of brand but also dedicating itself to ensuring its highly polished, media-agnostic solutions were rooted in evidence gained from research. From the start, the application of this formula led to some groundbreaking endeavors within the venerable automotive marketing segment, earning wide acclaim for the partnership's revolutionary impact on vehicle marketing. Through these sophisticated strategic collaborations, Scion landed more than half a million Scion buyers under the age of 35, ushered over 700,000 new buyers into the Toyota family, and sold over U.S. $20 billion-worth of vehicles.

Initially, to justify its surprising selection of ATTIK for Scion creative duties, Toyota pointed to the firm's design aesthetic and its strategic thinking. Validating that controversial move, ATTIK's patent creative approaches led to the focus on <u>personalization</u> as a primary marketing theme throughout the 14-year Scion experiment. That strategy – combined with painstaking design execution across all media channels – helped the manufacturer earn great returns on its investments.

There was another major client benefit ATTIK brought to the table: Based on the need to truly be effective for its clients, ATTIK's values embraced an impassioned level of hustling that truly set it apart from most of its competitors. As such, its principals were well versed in non-traditional media practices, many of which are credited with earning higher levels of trust among consumers compared with traditional approaches. The main types of non-traditional marketing activities include guerrilla/stealth/stunt/street marketing, participation in membership-based organizations, online events, parks and attractions, production placement, and tours and physical events.[4]

Within the Promotional Mix, non-traditional marketing typically falls under advertising. In ATTIK's hands, these types of activities were systematically enlisted to market vehicles in innovative ways.

Beginning by clearly identifying Scion's youth target as 18–35-year-old "urban trend leaders," ATTIK developed the brand's "look and feel" – as well as its Brand Guidelines – then began engaging with a world-class roster of media vendors to create and roll out an integrated, non-traditional "cross-media" ad campaign, while also relying on some extraordinary traditional media creative assets. Embracing its audience's overall aversion to being marketed to, ATTIK's pre-launch campaign for Scion's first two vehicles (the xA compact and the xB box) began by simply placing the vehicles in prominent positions at highly trafficked cultural events in California. From there, street team activities amped up the guerrilla message campaign in those initial markets, followed by TV spots, print ads, and some targeted PR efforts. The resulting buzz and media coverage played up the wide range of personalization options of the new vehicles, how and where they would be introduced, the simplified path to purchase, and the deep brand/dealer commitments to Scion's customers. Worth noting, in advance of activation, each of these campaign steps was run past focus groups and fine-tuned to address their feedback.

By design, what began as a regional campaign in California spread nationwide across America in June 2004, promoting the new tC sports coupe and the other models with new creative in virtually all media realms. These "Scion by" print, outdoor, television, and radio elements (each a unique execution featuring a creative individual's personal interpretation of what Scion meant to them) combined other campaign activities to deliver buzz marketing, event sponsorships, music tie-ins, a "branded entertainment" docudrama starring Scion's cars ... and countless other innovative promotions. Landing numerous creative industry awards and honors, the campaign proved effective in reaching trendsetting young men, firmly established the vehicles' "customizable" features in the minds of its target consumers and drove demand well beyond Toyota's production capacity.

This practical example of a very diligent, large-scale, sustained effort focused on selling cars to certain people is a superb example of marketing that was highly integrated. There was a traditional advertising component, but even those ads skewed more toward the lifestyle of the target audience than typical vehicle ads showing features and pricing. Also, the ads were only introduced after considerable non-traditional efforts were completed, and after calibrating all other aspects of The Promotional Mix toward the preferences of Scion's target audience.

I could go on and on, describing the diligence and care that went into every nuance of every activity and effort within The Promo Mix for Scion. Assessing them according to the brand values I have mentioned (bold, innovative thinking; magnificently authentic marketing; and customer reverence), the alignment was consistent year after year. As the legions of owners grew, Scion and ATTIK redoubled efforts to honor, move, motivate, and reward them ... all essentially in accordance with ATTIK's original 2002 Brand Guidelines.

Because of the importance of marketing authenticity, the clients encouraged ATTIK to shine the light on campaign efforts, and much of that was on my shoulders. If the campaign was introducing a music mixing microsite, an Augmented Reality app, a limited Release Series edition, a dealer event at Alcatraz Island, a massive owner gathering in the desert, a reality TV series, a non-traditional or even a traditional TV campaign, I was either being asked to get the word out, or to help with damage control. My work was done in concert with brand and agency leaders, and some brand PR managers and agency account directors I counted as Most Valuable Players.

Here is the takeaway from this download: Everything that client and agency marketers come up with across The Promo Mix is usually going to be spread out in front of a PR team to have them focus on the best ways to get the story out to the world. More specifically, that will come down to press releases and pitches designed to deliver earned – and sometimes, paid – media exposure ... and strategically sound Promo Mix activities across client- and/or agency-owned media channels, and those leveraged through media buys.

ISAM

Back in 2011, my clients at Leviathan joined together with some extremely talented colleagues to help the pioneering electronic musician and producer Amon Tobin and his record label, Ninja Tune, promote what would become one of the decade's biggest musical tour stories. Immediately after its premiere in Montreal, Adrian Covert of Gizmodo called it "the concert of the future, today."[5] In retrospect, to me, there were a few key aspects that made ISAM Live so phenomenal.

First, Mr. Tobin had a 15-year history of pushing the creative boundaries in sound recording, sound design, and music production as part of Ninja Tune, a London-based indie record label known for visionary innovation. With that ground situation, the expectations of anyone on the outside looking in were already extremely high.

The second essential ingredient is illuminated in a Beatport News interview with Mr. Tobin, where a question was asked about the challenge of realizing a singular vision as a live show.[6] In his response, Mr. Tobin explains how the ISAM visual spectacle came about as a means for solving a dilemma. Understanding that the record he had created was not a good fit for DJ sets in clubs, or for performance by musicians, he was challenged to create something special.

The solution resulted in two unique executions: an exquisite original art exhibition developed with artist Tessa Farmer called Control Over Nature, which appeared in London for a week after the debut of "ISAM" before travelling on to other cities like Paris and New York; and the mesmerizing spectacle he rolled out, which set him and "ISAM Live" apart in social media feeds around the world for the next several years.

So, the multifaceted solution that Mr. Tobin dreamt up for his problem was also of critical importance in how well the project was received. Finally, looking back at the historic achievements of ISAM, I give enormous credit to Ninja Tune for its masterful integrated marketing efforts. Nominated for the Association of Independent Music's Most Innovative Marketing Campaign of the Year ("Best Live Act," too) in 2011, the facets of the campaign, viewed on a timeline and assessed according to every lesson covered in this book, represent a best-case scenario. The content itself (ISAM, the album) was spectacular, and the artistic collaborations that introduced it to audiences matched that platinum standard in different realms of arts and entertainment, resulting in experiences that inspire rapture among audience members to this day. ISAM Live rode a "2.0" expansion all the way into 2015; to me, it was the brilliant campaign work of May 2011 – fully leveraging the combined Tobin/label superpowers, and Mr. Tobin's inventive approach to problem solving – that paved the way for all the commercial success.

My ISAM connection was through Leviathan, which partnered with V Squared Labs to create the original content in tandem with the groundbreaking projection mapping artistry for ISAM Live. Described as "a collaborative feat between the minds of madmen, scientists and visionaries," Leviathan's Matt Daly and his colleagues were widely acknowledged for their contributions, leading to many concerted marketing efforts between myself and Ninja Tune's leaders. Through those, we were able to shine more light on the players behind the scenes, and their magic in creating the must-see event that sold out every performance.

Even More Integrated Brilliance

Another campaign I had the opportunity to impact came through Foot Locker, Timberland, creative agency Pereira & O'Dell and creative production company Scholar. This partnership wisely turned to hip-hop legend Nas to authentically leverage the artist's life story in a set of animated ads released month after month in late 2017, in sync with the release of limited-edition series of Timberland boots at Foot Locker. This time, the setting – and the home field for marketing purposes – was Queens, New York, where the legend of Nas has played out, fueling pop culture worldwide for decades. Along with the eye-candy campaign videos featuring narration by Nas, which were used in TV, cable and online, there were also numerous out-of-home (billboard) executions, and in Foot Locker locations everywhere, in-store signage, special edition boxes, comic books and more.

In an interview with Adweek, Pereira & O'Dell's Executive Creative Director Dave Arnold confirmed that the campaign targeted 15- to 19-year-olds.[7] Further, he detailed the campaign's riveting focus on authenticity, which ensured all footwear shown in flashbacks was spot-on. Complementing other facets of The Promo Mix for this campaign, working through the agency's PR lead, we were able to bring more attention to the production company's work in creating the ads, and thereby amplify and extend the campaign messaging through our storytelling.

I also wanted to share an impressive report organized by marketing students at Central Michigan University including Michael Angelo Quiroz, who published the project on Medium in 2018.[8] Amazon is a brand that virtually all consumers have an ongoing relationship with, where the CX standards are consistently high, and for many, the engagement with the brand is 24/7. Mr. Quiroz and his colleagues astutely walked us through the company's history, its target audience, and its integrated marketing communications (IMC) objectives. Next, they explored The Promo Mix approaches, before assessing the overall efforts. Their score for Amazon: ten out of ten, based on the definition of IMC, and the net effects of its consistent, unified messaging.

There is one area where that otherwise stellar summary comes up a little short. Where they talk about the "type of agency" Amazon uses, they point out only the media agency responsible for buying and placing ads and promotions for the brand. That leaves out the creative agency, which for Amazon, begins with its in-house creative unit, D1. For the brand's star-studded 2018 Super Bowl spot dramatizing Alexa losing her voice, D1 teamed up with London agency Lucky Generals.[9] I am guessing that my ability to uncover that fact had everything to do with one or more PR professional who convinced Amazon's executives that it was worthwhile to share that information with the world. For a future Amazon Super Bowl spot, maybe you will be helping to get the story out, playing a part in sustaining the brand's mastery of IMC.

Exploration

1. If we view The Promo Mix as consisting of advertising, sales promotion, personal selling, direct and digital marketing, and PR, where does storytelling come in? In your answer, provide at least two examples.
2. Think about ways in which machine learning and automation might be applied to different areas of The Promo Mix and share a few of your ideas.
3. If it came to the world's attention that GEICO's CEO is living a lavish, flamboyant lifestyle, how do you think that might affect GEICO's business, which is so focused on saving money for its customers?
4. Imagine that you had to help ABC Entertainment explain to the world why the top-rated TV show in the country is being canceled. You must move quickly, and you have two sentences: Go.
5. One of ATTIK's big campaigns for Scion featured "Little Deviant" monsters who murdered Sheeple… all to introduce the new xD vehicle. What would be your first few talking points in justifying this creative approach to selling cars?

6. Why do you feel that non-traditional marketing tactics often carry more weight with consumers, compared with traditional marketing tactics?
7. Look up "ISAM Live" in Google Image Search. What do the images remind you of? In your opinion, what are the main things Amon Tobin achieved by pursuing his creative vision, and what role did marketing play in those achievements?
8. List five reasons why Nas was a good fit for a marketing campaign involving Timberland and Foot Locker. Also, why use animation for the campaign's visual elements?
9. Early on, Amazon focused on selling books, and customer reviews became extremely important to building trust among customers. List four other online businesses that have used online customer reviews to fortify their business. If one of those seems especially revolutionary to you, explain why.
10. For your personal favorite brand, pick one area of The Promo Mix where you feel that a new campaign effort could introduce significant benefits for the brand. Describe the campaign using the Copy Platform format (see chapter 4).

Notes

1 Belch, G., & Belch, M. (2021). *Advertising and Promotion: An Integrated Marketing Communications Perspective.* McGraw Hill.
2 Lynch, J. (2018, March 27). ABC Hopes Buyers Won't Judge Roseanne Based on Last Year's Disastrous Upfront Appearance. *Adweek.* https://adweek.it/2GwHqwZ.
3 Lynch, J. (2018, May 20). Inside Roseanne's Triumphant Return to TV. *Adweek.* https://adweek.it/2rLZHNY.
4 Non-Traditional Marketing. *Marketing-Schools.com.* http://bit.ly/ntmktg.
5 Covert, A. (2011, August 6). The Concert of the Future, Today. *Gizmodo.* http://bit.ly/FutNow.
6 Amon Tobin Interview. (2014 April 4). *Beatport News.* https://youtu.be/oxVVm75k_8Q.
7 Gianatasio, D. (2017, September 27). Nas Brings Street Cred to Effortlessly Cool Animated Ads for Timberland. http://adweek.it/2wVGf5X.
8 Beasley, B., Manning, B., Quiroz, M.A., & Rizkallah, J. (2018, March 12). Amazon.com's Integrated Marketing Communications. *Medium.com.* http://bit.ly/IMCamzn.
9 O'Brien, K. (2018, January 31). Ad of the Day: Alexa Loses Her Voice. *The Drum.* http://bit.ly/HiAlexa.

11
Cash Flow and Project Flow

As part of this process of illuminating the "big picture" of business, where we are ultimately aiming to establish the role of a communications consultant as an invaluable business partner with the maximum amount of job security, it is especially important to understand this: Any business can fail. What I want to accomplish here is to address the subject of business profitability – the financial metric underlying the cash flow issues blamed for most business failures – and provide some guidance for contributing to winning solutions. Also, I feel this is a good place to summarize PR Client Services activities in the context of project flow, so you can start to assess our toolset's capabilities against the more dire financial demands of a client company for yourself. One result of your due diligence on a potential client company could be you deciding to pass on it. On the other hand, by working with the company's leaders, you might become the person who helps right the ship and get it on track.

Profitability as a Business Objective

When I began outlining this book, cash flow is one of the top subjects I listed, for good reason. Essentially, several of my first professional experiences working in the entertainment industry were defined by my employers' shaky finances. There was a "no-budget" indie film where I dedicated my life for many weeks as a production coordinator and second assistant director; there, I drummed up over U.S. $50,000-worth of product placements but received no compensation. After that, there were two salaried positions – one in development, another as a writer – that led to lay-offs when those companies abruptly ran out of money.

From there, my luck improved, and by the time I was leaving TTG in LA to re-start Darnell Works, the opportunities I encountered were generally solid.

DOI: 10.4324/9781003177951-11

Still, a few came my way that triggered memories of dark days where overnight, trusted bosses had transformed into debtors who stopped returning my phone calls. Whether my instincts prove right or wrong, I have learned to listen for and trust them when meeting new business prospects and considering pledging my time to them.

As I flip back through the handful of new business opportunities I decided to pass on with little hesitation, is there a common characteristic? There is: In every case, the business either had no customers at all, or no regular customers. I do recommend following this lead generally, although I admit it rules out most startups, some of which could represent valuable opportunities for you. If you decide to bypass this qualification, at least consider Tacklebox Accelerator Founder Brian Scordato's advice, shared in a 2018 article in Fast Company.[1] By his account, of all the early-stage entrepreneurs his program engaged, all the most successful ones understood their purpose beyond their products; all could easily convey the impacts they would deliver for customers; and all conducted tests, collected data, then made analytical decisions.

For the record, being a financial mastermind is not a prerequisite for starting a business. Statistically, 20% of new businesses die in the first year; 50% last five years; and only 33% make it past ten years.[2] The common culprit behind their demise, most often, is the lack of profits.

Since this book aims to shine a spotlight on the ability to communicate complicated information in simple, meaningful ways, consider this: If running a successful business was easier, there would be at least twice as many of them. Who would profit from that? Certainly, the American Express Company might. According to Dun & Bradstreet, with over 70 million credit cards in circulation worldwide, American Express has U.S. $200 million in assets and bills U.S. $1.1 billion in business annually.[3] Obviously, it makes great sense for it to fund an educational website providing customers with insights, inspirations, and connections to help them do business. Unsurprisingly, the company's OPEN Forum is widely acknowledged as a quintessential example of *marketing as service*.

As evidence of OPEN Forum's aims to educate businesspeople about financial matters, one of its stories from writer Darren Dahl is entitled "Crunching the Numbers."[4] After making the point that running a successful company requires a positive cash flow, Mr. Dahl introduces Matt Fargo, the managing partner at Kurtz Fargo LLP and a mentor expert at the Boulder, Colorado-based startup accelerator, Boomtown. To Mr. Fargo, we read, the most imperative focus for entrepreneurs is to maintain vigilance regarding income and expenses. The article identifies many standard key performance indicators (KPIs), which may begin with tracking inventory over time. Other examples include cost per lead and conversion rate; customer retention, turnover, and complaints; customer online engagement level; growth rate; market share; order fulfillment cycle time; revenue growth; and/or revenue per employee.

I have largely built my career in the creative industry, and over time, I have learned enough about how businesses in this field operate to be able to navigate relatively successfully. Still, only ten percent of the companies I have worked with over the past 20 years are currently active on my client roster. That means there are more than 30 scenarios where a client moved on. Let's extract some insights from this archive which you can use to advantage.

Among the most accomplished business professionals I know, many refer to former Harvard Business School professor David H. Meister's seminal book, *Managing the Professional Service Firm*, as gospel. Based on my experience, if this book was required reading for someone launching a new company, I would expect the number of startups to dwindle. The adage about ignorance being bliss comes to mind, and the one that begins, "if I knew then what I know now…." What does Mr. Meister write about cash flow? Very little. However, the entire third chapter is devoted to profitability. And while I do not doubt the validity of his discussions on "profit per partner," at least to me, they get somewhat complicated.

To better comprehend business finance with Mr. Meister's help, his opening comments from his book's very first chapter are enlightening. Writing out the mission statement behind every professional service firm he ever encountered, it appears each one is dedicated to impeccable customer service, helping its people grow and satisfy career aims, and to financial success.[5] This truly does cover the basic mission of most of the clients I have engaged with, which is telling: Financial success is a primary objective for them all. When things are going well, a company's employees, partners, and contractors can focus on doing their jobs; importantly, making money is an imperative … so helping your clients fulfill that part of their mission is essential, even if it is never mentioned.

Navigating Financial Challenges

When it comes to how I structure my client business arrangements, my standard approaches tend to follow in the footsteps of Michael Terpin at TTG. While there, many potential client companies offered to compensate us in stock. To the best of my knowledge, Mr. Terpin only agreed to accept U.S. dollars. For my part, requesting to be paid upfront and in actual money in my terms of engagement has resulted in losing some potential clients. All things considered, I am willing to accept the losses, knowing those companies may have had trouble paying me, which was bound to add friction to an already high-pressure relationship.

Next, every TTG client was on retainer, and no company was ever handled on a project basis; I have generally adopted these tenets as well. Early on, out of necessity, I tried a few small projects for tiny fees to build up my experience. If you find yourself in the same position and decide to forge ahead, you are sure to learn something. There is much more to know about bidding, winning, and managing accounts. Right now, I will say this: In my experience, aiming high has often been rewarded. Within the past few years, a fellow communications consultant asserted that clients who pay more are often much easier to deal with. On the flip side, it is surprising how often companies that engage for less money are harder to please. That is more reinforcement for me to not engage clients on a project basis, where the spend is less and assessing their financial stability more difficult. No doubt, it is a luxury to have better paying clients, but it is also well worth the effort to set high standards in how you do business, and to make yourself worthy of a monthly retainer.

Taking all this information into account, a framework appears for ideal clients, engagement structures and working relationships: The clients are stable enough to be able to afford a communications consultant relatively easily; they are willing to accept terms that include paying a monthly retainer in advance; and the work to be done is both fairly obvious and relevant to the company's bottom-line business success. Fortunately for me, I can usually look at the media coverage I have helped my clients generate as the validation for their payments to me. Even in the scenario where the clients are stellar and we fit together perfectly, over time, financial difficulties can still arise.

Turning once again to David C. Baker of ReCourses, in his highly recommended book *Financial Management of a Marketing Firm*, he gets extremely specific about cash flow. Of course, this level of counsel is relevant to you in your consulting business – and to the leadership of your client companies.

> To avoid cash flow difficulty, maintain an appropriate cushion, manage your growth carefully and pay as you grow, build extra cushion if you have a client-concentration issue, keep a tight rein on accounts payable, adjust your overhead in a timely fashion, put embezzling controls in place, and create a culture of appropriate financial reporting. Then you'll be all set.[6]

Cash Flow and Project Flow

This provides a set of guidelines for you to be wary of as your client relationships proceed over time. If there are consistent delays in receiving your pay, if you hear grumbling about clients or vendors that have to do with payments, if you witness workplace inefficiency on a scale that seems troublesome ... those are just some of the signs that a client company may have problems that could impact your future. In any of those situations, you have a decision to make: Do you jump ship, or do you try to be part of the solution?

Here, I will introduce what I call Darnell's Law: "Every new development, good or bad, is half challenge and half opportunity." Adopting this hard-earned lesson demands a commitment to examining occurrences beyond the surface, and to being prepared to act when unforeseen circumstances arise. It surpasses simply being a proactive, strategic communicator for a client company, which is sure to be your primary role; owning this mindset can make you more resilient and allow you to help solve problems in ways that are highly likely to exceed client expectations.

When those problems are of a financial nature, the prospect of you surviving the first round of cutbacks is slim. Through vigilance in monitoring the health of your client company, and preparedness, swift action and savvy communications efforts can position you as a chief navigator of troubled waters. By applying the world-class skill set at the heart of this book (delivering focused expertise in the fields of Account Management, Customer Service, Planning, Writing, Media Relations, Measurement and Reporting), you can quickly leap into the processes necessary to understand exactly where a business stands, move through the steps to reestablish financial stability, and rebuild for the present and the future.

To guide those business-saving endeavors, I point you to the Nolo Network – an expansive and free library of legal information – and attorney and legal editor Bethany K. Laurence. Here are two articles to read that quickly lead you from the big picture understanding of why difficulties can arise from nowhere, through to the strategic and tactical efforts necessary for survival.

- Saving a Money-Losing Business with a Business Survival Plan: http://bit.ly/NOLOrx1
- How to Cut Costs and Spend Less in a Cash-Strapped Business: http://bit.ly/NOLOrx2

In that last article, Ms. Laurence provides an insight that easily justifies the role of a shrewd, agile, intelligent communicator even in the leanest of times. What she asserts is this: A drop in sales is the signal to step marketing efforts up, not down. She also adds, considering profitability, it is probably wiser to focus on lower cost, non-traditional campaign efforts that focus on engaging key customers in supporting your business.[7]

By now, you know a lot about the types of efforts and techniques she is suggesting. Let's walk through what I see as the main types of project flows likely to structure the actual work involved in delivering vital results for your clients.

Project Flows

When explaining how I set up my client relationships, I have mentioned only working with companies on an ongoing basis, where we have an agreement in place stating that if things go well, we will continue until one party decides to end the engagement. Specifically, I have made the case against working on a project-basis, where I might be hired to handle a single assignment. I explain this to clarify my suggestions on how to structure client relationships, but also to make this point: The work you are hired to do for your clients is certain to come down to projects.

Even in the best-case scenario, you will be handling at least one project at a time, and the hope is that you will be able to consistently deliver returns on your clients' investments that certify your value to the organization and make you essential for as long as reasonably possible. Here are some tips on becoming an expert project manager.

In the creative industry, producers are usually the project managers, and for important developments, I have seen that executive producers are usually very hands-on. A typical project will start with the bid phase, and in the winning cases, it will then be awarded. From there, planning focuses on pre-production, production, post-production, and delivery ... possibly followed by some internal development to create case studies and handle award submissions. All projects occur over a span of time, and the producer's job is to understand the tasks involved in delivering the finished project, and to coordinate or allocate resources over the available amount of time to meet the deadline for delivery.

The Project Management Triangle is well known in many realms where customers are seeking services and the vending company wants to properly register expectations.[8] It is customarily presented like so: "Good, Fast or Cheap: Pick Two." If the desire is to limit spending, you can often either have it good or fast, but not both. All the other variations based on this

Cash Flow and Project Flow 113

framework also have a good chance of being applicable. This is a strong reminder of how important time becomes in the delivery of virtually any type of service.

The time aspect of project management is so important that there is a vital organizational tool in wide use whose primary function is to allow progress to be visualized over time using a horizontal scale. Introduced by H.L. Gantt about a century ago, Gantt charts are essential in project management. You can learn more about them and their use in this YouTube video from Project Management Videos.

- How to Use Gantt Charts: https://youtu.be/LrtLig0yYrs

This example of such a chart from the planning phase of a big client campaign very quickly communicates when certain developments are scheduled to occur, so that everyone involved can aim to be on the same page at the right times.

Just as being financially successful is always an imperative for any business, completing its projects on time and at the highest standard attainable is the life blood of any service business. For companies that develop products, the

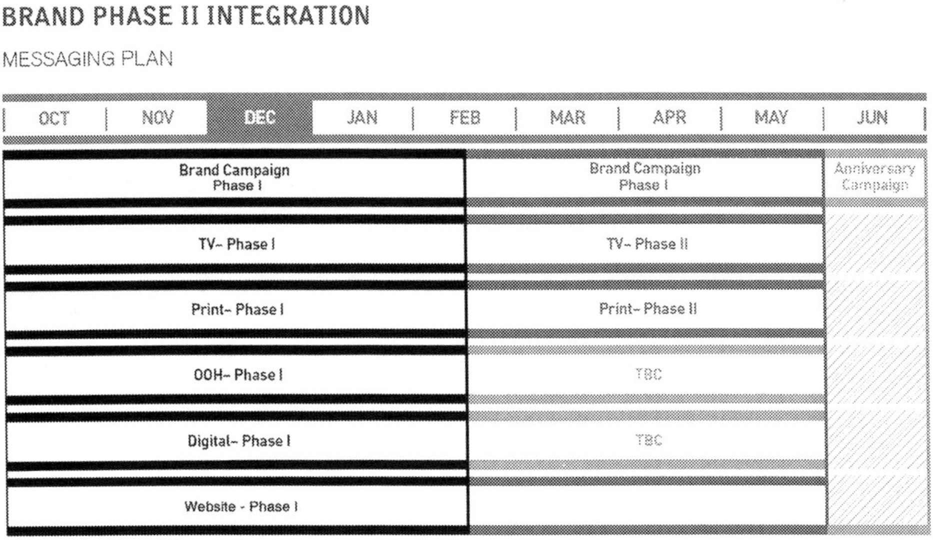

BRAND PHASE II INTEGRATION
MESSAGING PLAN

OCT	NOV	DEC	JAN	FEB	MAR	APR	MAY	JUN
Brand Campaign Phase I				Brand Campaign Phase I			Anniversary Campaign
TV- Phase I				TV- Phase II			
Print- Phase I				Print- Phase II			
OOH- Phase I				TBC			
Digital- Phase I				TBC			
Website - Phase I							

Figure 4 Campaign Messaging Plan.

tasks and workplace functions can be considerably different ... yet they are still driven by the organization and allocation of resources over periods of time, aimed at meeting optimal performance levels and measures of quality.

For the communications consultant, the assignments will either be handed out specifically, or it will be your job to survey everything happening within a company to the best of your ability, and then to propose projects. Your understanding of leadership, business objectives, brands, branding, sales, customer service, and integrated marketing all needs to come together, especially focusing on whatever goals or objectives your lead puts in front of you. Here are a few examples of projects likely to fit.

1. A press release or article documenting a big recent project where your client's client is highly pleased, with all the research necessary to gain either the most high-profile media exposure, or wide exposure that reaches as much of the target audience as possible ... and having that content play out across the company's owned media channels on a timely basis.
2. A press release about one or more important new hires for the company.
3. A communications audit that helps the company assess its full communications capabilities and manage them brilliantly and effectively, in line with its overall corporate objectives.

You get the idea. From here, spend a little time thinking about managing such projects. When you have established a monthly retainer to work within and know how many hours that affords you, it will be up to you to determine what work needs to be done (researching, proposing plans, more research for developing content, writing, coordinating media assets, securing client permissions, pitching, tracking, reporting) and then scheduling your activities with the goals of delivering your assignments on time, staying on budget, and ensuring your clients are pleased with your efforts.

There are essential contributions you can make to your clients' businesses, in good times and in challenging ones. Even with limited experience, I became a highly effective alchemist in this realm, constantly working in strategic and tactical ways to be able to ensure I was worthy of the retainer, and that my clients would want and be able to stick with me. By being savvy to profitability, and capable of contributing to a company's financial success – and simultaneously learning to manage project flows effectively as part of your ongoing client relationships – you will be in solid position to build a career that is independent and sustainable.

Exploration

1. Why is it smart to assess a potential client company's project needs and its financial strengths prior to beginning a relationship with them?
2. How can you justify being paid a monthly retainer in advance? (Answer: It is widely considered "industry standard" for PR professionals to be paid in advance.)
3. Imagine your client company must lay off key employees. What can you do to convince the leaders that it is wise to keep you onboard?
4. Your check is late in arriving 3 months in a row. Describe how you would respond to your client company – and what steps you might make in the future if the problem persists.
5. A client is late in paying your retainer, but you have no choice but to continue working. Suddenly you learn they need to terminate you. Share the key aspects of your initial response to your client.
6. As part of an important project, you learn that the client's clients are displeased. What can you do to ensure the matter gets the proper attention, and/or to positively impact the client relationship to everyone's benefit?
7. One of your best clients experiences a rough patch and needs to take a hiatus or cut their retainer. How do you respond?
8. A former retainer client returns and asks you to consider handling a project. What do you say?
9. If you have clients that are primarily service based, when is the best time for you to get involved in their projects, for PR purposes, and why? How about for clients that develop products?
10. I often tell my clients that there is little point in trying to do PR on a project until their client is happy – and sometimes, that day never arrives. Explain why you agree or disagree with this. Also, bear this in mind: Waiting to launch a PR effort does not necessarily mean you cannot begin project planning and research, to prepare yourself to leap into action when the client love manifests.

Notes

1 Scordato, B. (2018, July 10). The Ultimate Checklist for Predicting Early-Stage Startups' Success. *Fast Company*. http://f-st.co/cZDzbs6.
2 Speights, K. (2017, May 3). What Percentage of Businesses Fail in Their First Year? *The Motley Fool*. http://bit.ly/2p8rGDe.
3 Company Profile: American Express Company. (n.d.). *Dun & Bradstreet*. Retrieved February 28, 2021, from http://bit.ly/DBAmEx.

4 Dahl, D. (2015, August 31). Crunching the Numbers. Boomtown: Think Like a Startup. *Boomtown Accelerators.* https://boomtownaccelerators.com/crunching-the-numbers/.
5 Maister, D.H. (1997). *Managing the Professional Service Firm* (Rev. ed.). Free Press.
6 Baker, D.C. (2010). *Financial Management of a Marketing Firm.* RockBench Publishing Corp.
7 Laurence, B.A.K. (2014, November 18). *How to Cut Costs and Spend Less in a Cash-Strapped Business.* Nolo. http://bit.ly/NOLOrx2.
8 Wikipedia contributors. (2020, September 1). Project management triangle. Wikipedia. https://en.wikipedia.org/wiki/Project_management_triangle.

Part 3

Communications Consulting

Topics Covered

The Communications Consultant in Practice   *119*
Consistencies and Variations by Client Size   *129*
Media and Its Usage   *140*
My Version and Your Version   *151*
Is Consulting Right for You?   *156*

12
The Communications Consultant in Practice

When Pamela Tuscany engaged me to write news releases for Century III at Universal Studios Florida (C3), I had my first taste of being a professional communications consultant. I recall that when I heard about the opportunity through a friend, it was described like so: "Century III is looking for a writer." There was a bit more detail about organizing press releases, but at its heart, it was a writing job. Among the many different types of work I was doing at that time, this was the gig that intrigued me the most, despite the low pay. When I was sitting in the lobby of the extremely impressive facility, walking through the corridors or the plush editing suites with Ms. Tuscany or any of the other executives, I really felt like somebody. In a matter of weeks, everyone seemed to know what I was doing there, and I could sense their appreciation for me bringing their stories into the world.

There are many aspects to operating as a communications consultant. Once more, here is what I consider to be the key skill set: Account Management; Customer Service; Planning; Writing; Media Relations; Measurement; Reporting.

- For more insights into what makes a successful "planner" in the world of advertising agencies, check out this article from Leo Burnett USA's EVP Head of Planning, Nic Chidiac: http://bit.ly/1TiwfU9.[1]

My C3 experiences involved all these skills, except for media relations. It took a few more years for me to attain the knowledge that would add that important facet to my capabilities. I have also discussed the efforts I put into submitting my creative writing to literary publications; when I switched over to writing nonfiction stories for trade media outlets, my placement percentage improved exponentially, and I even started making a little money that way. In the bigger picture, I was building my expertise in interfacing

DOI: 10.4324/9781003177951-12

with gatekeepers in the media, learning what interested them, and how the process of interfacing with them worked to get them copy, images, and other media assets. When I landed at Crest National in Hollywood, I made the case for being adept at media relations, and thankfully I was able to substantiate that right away. In summary, that culmination of attaining the key skill set occurred while I was an employee. Although I was increasingly confident in applying my knowledge in the film and TV production and post-production industries, the education I earned by working with Tim Street and his colleagues at The Spark Factory, and then at TTG, represented the rocket fuel that took me to the next levels. Specifically, applying my talents to a creative production outfit focused on network television promotions as director of marketing made me appreciate all aspects of marketing, while also helping me understand how the communications or the PR role could have a massive impact on a tight budget. And at TTG, along with a small team of colleagues where we all possessed the key skill set, together we were attracting nearly U.S. $100,000 in monthly billings.

Worth mentioning here is that TTG was a specialized PR agency known for its expertise in high-tech. You have not yet heard me mention the term "publicist," although any definition for a communications consultant is sure to closely resemble that well-known profession. The differences are subtle but important. In my experience, PR professionals from the high-tech sector of the business world command higher pay than most publicists do. While those who operate as publicists do similar work, I view a communications consultant as having the responsibility to be more of a planner and a writer, and someone who is more deeply immersed in a company's overall marketing strategy, versus mainly focusing on publicity. With all due respect to the world's publicists, who do such great work for entertainment projects, celebrities and vital institutions like restaurants and travel destinations, my focus with this training goes to a deeper level, at least in my opinion. Certainly, great publicists operate at deep strategic levels and are highly valuable; largely, we all share the same end goals. If establishing yourself as a publicist is your aim, I expect this curriculum to serve you well.

The DWA came to be in 2000 in Los Angeles, and due to me attaining the key skill set and having demonstrated success applying it for businesses, when I put myself out there professionally and pursued clients, I soon had a roster of companies to serve. In the years since, that has been the basic description of my career situation. Although we have moved twice during this time into different markets, the business has held up. The roster has changed, and I have had to hustle to stay sharp, and to ensure I am continuing to bring value to each of my clients. To help you better understand exactly what this consists of, let's analyze a client relationship that began in 2011 and has survived over time, with lots of twists and turns along the way.

Arc of a DWA Relationship

Throughout my tenure serving as PR agency of record for specialized creative agency Leviathan, the company has usually been one of five roster clients, and our budget has run from U.S. $3,500 to $1,500 per month, with the occasional month "off." From the beginning, the approximately 20-person shop has occupied an impressive space in Chicago's Fulton Market District, and based on my work with other similar companies, I was drawn in right away by the warmth and confidence of company CEO Chad Hutson. One of the big insights I have observed is that it is good to be contacted by someone who is not the company's legitimate leader – but when the CEO or President is the one calling me, that is even better. The reasons are obvious: Over time, even the most trusted employees will move on. All things considered, to me, building one's relationship with the leader is the best-case scenario.

I always start building my clients' communications toolset by focusing on positioning. Across our first six years of diligence, Leviathan's shifted significantly. I think it is safe to say that Leviathan's early growth hit some speed bumps, scaling up and back down at times, based on changes among its clientele and their marketplaces. But overall, the business grew, leading to its 2017 acquisition by an outside investor group, which added stability and led to success at higher levels.

Looking back, as the nature of the company's client engagements changed, so did the focus expressed in our messaging. When I talk to my clients about finding the right positioning language, I always set out to solve the challenge to the best of our abilities for this moment, and use that language across all our communication channels; from there, we are always ready to change when necessary. I give full credit to Mr. Hutson for staying on his toes in this department and following my counsel to the letter by proactively leading the way forward.

- 2011: Leviathan is a design-focused production studio specializing in the creation of large-scale visual experiences across all media.
- 2013: Leviathan is a creative studio that crafts animated content and immersive installations for brands, agencies, and entertainers worldwide.
- 2014: Leviathan is a conceptual design company that creates engaging narrative content and experiences for brands and entertainers worldwide.

- 2016: Leviathan is a specialized creative agency that crafts enduring experiences through the seamless integration of premium content, innovative interactivity, and physical environments.
- 2019: Leviathan is a specialized creative agency that transforms distinctive environments into exceptional experiences.

By the numbers, we put out an average of seven news releases per year covering major projects, staff additions, and other milestone developments. One of the things I had learned working for other creative entities was that very often with a project story, there also was a video ... usually a commercial, or perhaps a "Making Of" or "Behind the Scenes" video. Early into our relationship, Leviathan set a new standard in producing "Case Study" videos of extraordinary quality. Those helped us exponentially in our media relations efforts, providing an asset representing a newsworthy hook for publications, even when the core project had made its splash weeks or months earlier. In the news business where timing is everything, this advantage is vital. Combining Leviathan's original videos with the news releases I assembled using in-depth executive input, the media coverage we earned was consistently solid. Highlights included coverage in *The Chicago Tribune*, *Creativity*, *The Creators Project*, *Fast Company*, *Gizmodo*, *The Los Angeles Times*, *Motionographer*, and *WIRED*, among many others; award recognition from the AICP, the Association of Independent Music, *Communication Arts* magazine, *Event Marketer*, *Motionographer*, The One Club, and the Themed Entertainment Association; and invaluable co-op marketing ventures through industry software leaders Autodesk, Derivative, Epic Games, and Maxon.

The flow of information over time prioritized important projects in the pipeline, the addition of new talents, and company involvement in external events, including executive speaking engagements. The team consistently updated their web presence to keep them on the leading edge compared with their top competitors, and we also worked together to ensure that the best of our clients', partners', key players', and the company's latest developments all were cross-promoted regularly on Leviathan's social media channels. I am also proud to say that at the time we began, public speaking engagements were high on the wish list for company executives. Together, we were able to shape up more than 50 significant opportunities, ranging from local to international.

This is just one example of one client relationship. The next chapters in this section will talk about some general variations on the role of a communications consultant by client size, more specifics about media assets, and a summary comparison between how my business works and how yours might. I am

Roles and Responsibilities of the PR Champion

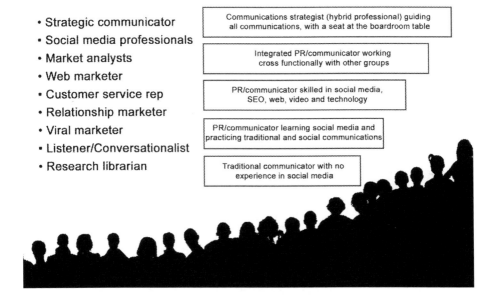

Figure 5 Roles and Responsibilities of the PR Champion.[2]

sure you can see already how these illustrations used by author and business luminary Deirdre Breakenridge to help educate PR professionals about the profession apply to the work I have performed for Leviathan.

DWA Closer to Home

Among many cool people around the world, I am especially indebted to the executives who made global creative agency ATTIK so successful. Way back in 2003, at the impassioned encouragement of VP of Business Development and Marketing Lisa Cleff-Kurtz, ATTIK U.S. President and Group Sales Director Will Travis took a chance by engaging me to handle PR for his San Francisco-based operation. Within a couple of years, Mr. Travis returned to New York City to reestablish ATTIK there, and by that time, Ric Peralta had been named Global CEO for the agency. With offices on America's West and East Coasts, and in northern England, these executives put their trust in me, working from my home office in quiet, pastoral settings in North Carolina's Blue Ridge Mountains. My relationships with those individuals remain close to this day.

I am living proof that technology now allows us to do our work from anywhere. What I wrote in the chapter on Strategy remains true today: Since

Communications Consulting

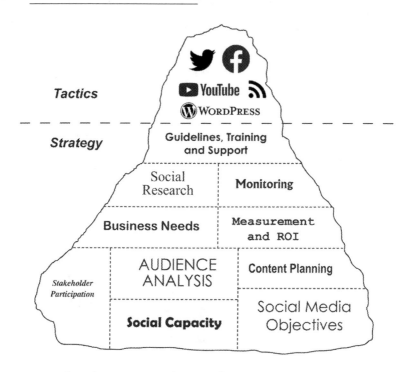

Figure 6 Social Media Strategy and Tactics.[3]

2000, I have dedicated myself to being extraordinary at my job for each of my roster clients, and to keeping my roster small, to allow me to fulfill that objective. This translates into an average monthly retainer of at least U.S. $12,000. At many times I have consistently operated closer to U.S. $17,000 per month. That has everything to do with how well I work with the particular clients – and the impact of the overall group dynamic of the entire roster on my schedule.

What I have been so fortunate to find, thanks in large part to Mrs. Cleff-Kurtz, Mr. Travis, Mr. Peralta, and Mr. Hutson, is that when I deliver extraordinary service to my clients, not only do they want to continue to work with me ... they also refer me to others, especially if I alert them when I am looking for a new client. That approach of serving my key evangelists, focusing on them, and calling on them for help when I need it, has been so successful that I have never needed to advertise my business, nor expend much energy pursuing sales. Generally, I tend to have enough clients, and regularly attract multiple referrals each month.

Back in 2000, I obsessed over keeping my roster intact, and when I was contacted by someone about handling PR for their company, I usually just referred them – often without speaking – to other top PR pros. I eventually came to appreciate that when those calls occur, I am in a unique position to make a new friend, and potentially, a new business partner, even if we do not hook up immediately. The practice I have adopted over the past several years has been to set up a call with anyone who reaches out, if only to meet them, hear them out on their needs, share some free advice that is honest and endearing, and attempt to attract them as a future client. I also keep records of those inquiries, and when I have an opening, I circle back to those contacts. That list is also used at Thanksgiving time each year, when I send a note to my clients, friends, and other VIPs to express my gratitude for them.

This approach keeps me where I want to be most of the time. I also make it a practice to arrange a trip to spend some face time with new clients within the first month or two of engaging, if possible. Almost all client work can be done remotely, in my experience, but even a little time spent in person goes a long way toward building meaningful relationships. When I was in LA working at TTG, we would always go spend time meeting with prospective clients even before pitching them. Nowadays, those initial meetings are done by Zoom or telephone.

Despite my best efforts, there have been times when I have dropped below my quota of clients ... and more than once, I have had two clients depart simultaneously. That occurred coming into both 2014 and 2016, with little warning either time. In 2012, a longstanding client informed me they were dropping me while we were in the middle of our family vacation. If it is not abundantly clear already, this is a complex job, and each client represents its own universe. While the rewards are great, there is significant risk. For me, the disappointments received by phone or email have prompted some additional efforts, aimed at attracting potential clients in ways that fit with my customer-first service strategy.

Since I consider myself to be a writer and artist at my core, I have drawn a lot of inspiration from Julia Cameron's great book, *The Artist's Way*. Her guidance allowed me to put the spotlight on myself, my interests, and my personal development, in ways I had never imagined. Through her teaching – and by recalling that when I was at TTG, one of my colleagues handled PR for the firm itself – I finally realized the need to handle my own business as though it's a roster client. This idea came to the forefront in conjunction with the rise of social media, and it became even more involved when I updated my website in 2014. Suddenly, I was obliged to regularly write content for my blog, post items on social media, and update my website ... all to ensure that those who find my content encounter my expertise and learn more about my services.

August 2017 was a month when I found myself below my client quota. Another key requirement for my business is timekeeping; my diligence is recorded faithfully, and those records constitute the reports I deliver at the end of each period to substantiate my work. I also record charges for the time I spend serving my own business. That month, when my revenue was below my target, I spent almost three hours per day serving myself; that includes pursuing new clients, but also, developing content that appears in this book.

In the early days of your consultancy, and in challenging times when changes present themselves, you will find that your priorities are consumed by sales and marketing. My efforts in adding those types of actions into my day-to-day operations have served me well in such times, while also allowing me to remain primarily focused on my standard priorities: the clients on my roster.

An Executive's Summary

I find priceless wisdom in Marty Nemko's *Time* magazine article where he shares a list identifying these mainstays of job satisfaction: Work that is not too hard or too easy; work that feels worthy and ethical; a boss that treats you well; coworkers you enjoy; moderate opportunities for learning; reasonable work hours; reasonable pay; reasonable benefits; job security; a reasonable commute.[4]

If we started at the end of that list, I think my scenario wins the prize. Since leaving TTG in 2000, I have worked in my home office … and as our children grew into teenagers, the days when I did not see them were extremely rare. Proceeding from the bottom of that list upwards, I feel my job has been about as secure as any. Certainly, I have had to commit myself to improving and learning new things, but all that knowledge and expanded skill set is mine to use and leverage, moving forward. A case could be made that the benefits are very hard-earned (working hours can frequently be hard to limit… and in chapter 16, I will discuss the high costs and low perks of insurance), but considering that my wife was able to stay home and not earn a paycheck for our first 14 years as parents, that I get holidays off, that we have taken multiple vacations every year since 2000 and even took an entire month off in the summer of 2012 (and still took spring and holiday breaks that year, too), I've found the benefits of this profession to be opulent.

My 2021 hourly rate was U.S. $215 per hour. Given all the details shared in this summary, I have no complaints about the working hours. While I can imagine many professions where the work is rote and repetitive, in this one, the learning curve is constant, and I value the fact that I am often being paid to learn. Although my coworkers are almost all remote from my location, my wife has played a vital role as sounding board, confidante, chief advisor, and chief financial officer throughout my self-employment.

Next comes the idea of having a boss that treats one well. While this has proven to be the case for me 95% of the time, I have persevered under some situations that were not great, and I have also ended a few relationships that caused me to lose a lot of sleep. The ability to handle those situations according to my choosing is another lovely benefit of operating a business with multiple clients and revenue streams, where referrals arrive regularly. Obviously, that also bears on situations where my work might not feel worthy or ethical; having some control empowers me to shoot straight with my clients and myself.

Atop the Nemko list is having a job where the work is reasonably challenging. Happily, I can report that I am extremely proud of my work as a communications consultant serving my clients.

Exploration

1. List the various aspects of the key skill set for a communications consultant. Which area seems easiest to gain proficiency in, and which seems most difficult?
2. For another example of an astute individual applying the key skill set to something very practical, read this story from publicity expert Joan Stewart entitled "How to Publicize a Garden Walk and Other Local Events": http://ow.ly/pOhH30dHOuv[5]
3. Think about the areas of business that interest you and identify five experts who handle PR or publicity in those realms. Are they listed as Publicists, PR professionals, or something else?
4. In the research for question three, do you have any sense of what sets the Publicist(s) apart from the other professionals you found? If so, list a few.
5. Describe a nonfiction story you could write yourself, about something that is of interest to you, that you could envision appearing in a publication. Explain your strategy for pitching it, who you would pitch it to, and what you could add to make it more interesting (for example, pictures, an illustration, a video).
6. When your efforts in question five play out, there will be a story that appears. What do you do to bring that story to a wider audience?
7. If you have a sense of operating as a business, what are ten keywords that help define what is most unique about you and the services you provide?

If you are unclear, research Joan Stewart from question two above, and enter ten keywords for her.
8. Identify five businesses you would love to have on your roster if you already were a consultant. For the ten keywords identified in question seven, what additional keywords could you add to better attract the types of businesses you wish to work with?
9. Now, do enough homework to identify two different companies or entrepreneurs who you think you could contact about doing work for them. These can come from your personal network, or from searching through job listings (like this one: https://twitter.com/i/lists/823101).
10. Look at the economic situation you currently face in your life. If you were considering taking a low-paying job for one year specifically to earn experience you could leverage as a consultant for years to come, what is the minimum pay you could accept?

Notes

1 Chidiac, N. (2016, May 17). Four Things to Look for in Planners Today. *Leo Burnett*. http://bit.ly/1TiwfU9.
2 Breakenridge, D. (2012, February 13). Please Recommend a #PR 2.0 Champion. *Deirdre Breakenridge*. https://www.deirdrebreakenridge.com/please-recommend-a-pr-2-0-champion.
3 Smiciklas, M. (2012). Social Media Strategy and Tactics. https://intersectionconsulting.com.
4 Nemko, M. (2014, October 13). Why Following Your Passion Is the Worst Kind of Career Advice. *Time*. http://bit.ly/TimeMNem.
5 Stewart, J. (2017, July 27). How to Publicize a Garden Walk and Other Local Events. *The Publicity Hound*. https://bit.ly/ink4GW.

13
Consistencies and Variations by Client Size

In the previous chapter, I shared an illustration from author and business luminary Deirdre Breakenridge, where she identifies common roles and responsibilities for "PR Champions." This comes from her 2009 book, co-authored with Brian Solis, entitled *Putting the Public Back in Public Relations*. Every moment I have spent with Ms. Breakenridge and her content has proven to be extremely valuable – so I recommend you bookmark https://www.deirdrebreakenridge.com and visit often. In those illustrations, several service levels are identified, where the first describes a hybrid, professional communications strategist, the second is a communicator who works in various functions across different groups, and the third is a communicator skilled in social media, search engine optimization (SEO), web, video, and technology.

Based on my own experience, I have taken the liberty of regrouping functions and roles for our purposes, and I have also reshuffled them. These classifications will guide us in exploring how the job of a communications consultant can work in various situations based on small, medium, and large company sizes. To clarify a bit, while my clients have generally had fewer than 30 employees, the U.S. Small Business Administration defines any company with fewer than 500 employees as a small business. So, although my discussions are primarily focused on companies with up to 200 employees, I will also share some notes about how communications consultants can contribute positive impacts to larger institutions.

Universal Consistencies

Here again is our key skill set for this profession: Account Management; Customer Service; Planning; Writing; Media Relations; Measurement; Reporting. From there, here is what I consider to be the full set of PR

DOI: 10.4324/9781003177951-13

functions that apply to every client situation any of us will encounter. It is presented with the lead roles at the top.

- Analyst and Historian: You begin by listening and learning; over time, by stepping into each of the following roles, you become a (or "the") keeper of the company's history.
- Strategist and Chief Communications Officer (CCO): Viewing the company in all its glory from the top down, you call shots and deal with consequences to help drive success. Sometimes the closest you can come to this role is Chief Ally to the CCO.
- Patron of Sales: Supporting sales is typically your most important job.
- Patron of Customer Service: If a company's products or its services fail, it is doomed.
- Relationship Developer: The positive results of sales and service have people behind them: You will be their champion in cultivating and harvesting those happy, healthy relationships.
- Storyteller: Without the support of the above functions, the only stories you can tell are make-believe. Authentic storytelling requires deep understanding and quality ingredients, for starters.
- Marketing Maven: To be effective, marketing must promote promises that can be fulfilled. Only by diligently researching the company, its offerings and its audience can we develop viable marketing frameworks capable of consistently delivering positive results. Worth noting here – up-to-date knowledge of integrated marketing is extremely advantageous.

Going back several years, I had an interview with Don McNeill, the co-founder, CEO, and executive chairman at creative experience company Digital Kitchen (DK), who introduced a framework that I have referenced ever since. I am not sure what he called it, but I refer to it as the McNeill PR Triangle. As we were discussing DK's PR needs at that time, he told me that from his point of view, PR came down to three things: (1) the work; (2) a company's efforts to communicate with its PR partner; and (3) the capabilities of that PR partner. He then went on to assign a letter grade to each of those areas in assessing DK's recent performance. When he told me that he felt they needed work on item two, I could instantly see how that was the obvious pathway to improving their results.

Another thing I like about the McNeill PR Triangle is this: There are two key aspects of generating the desired results which are mostly in others' hands. That is not to say that a skilled communications consultant cannot have an impact on a company's work ... it is just that, most often, the work is already completed, and the company is looking to generate buzz with it, by the time it is put in front of the PR partner. The second aspect – having to do with a company's efforts to communicate to its PR partner – can be impacted by the PR leader's research methodology and willingness to do whatever is necessary to become educated. However, I have seen that an emphasis on PR from the top of organizations is required to build the fire necessary to make communications processes effective.

Assuming the client company has great new work to share, and that its talents are aligned around ensuring that its PR partner is provided everything necessary to succeed, the last piece of the equation is represented by the PR partner's capabilities. These include the mastery of research, storytelling, media relations, marketing and other arts and sciences illuminated through this training – but there is also the vitally important element of time, which is often affected by budget. All the capabilities must be put into effect in a way that leads to results within a reasonable amount of time and budget, to demonstrate that the relationship is sound and sustainable. My companion book thoroughly drills into account management. Here, just bear in mind that when it comes to applying ourselves as communications consultants, the clock is always running, and when we perform well, most of those minutes need to translate into revenues for us and for our clients.

Liaisons

After working with one company for about eight years, where my liaison changed out annually and the latest of those shake-ups was still playing out, I was befriended by the consultant they brought in to help with management. After surveying the entire staff, she reported back to tell me she had not found a single person who said it was their job to communicate with me on a regular basis. This was a top client for me, and while the situation was alarming, I also saw it as an opportunity, per Darnell's Law.

- Every new development, good or bad, is half challenge and half opportunity.

My epiphany in that situation alerted me to an essential aspect of each of my business relationships, which I had never fully understood. Every client relationship comes down to the person – or sometimes a group of people – at a company who take responsibility for making my relationship effective. While I never took those vital connections for granted, the lesson is one I now emphasize in new client relationships. I always favor business partnerships where the owner is the person reaching out to me; now you know why.

If the person running the show is committed to leveraging PR, I have a better expectation that I will get what I need, and my contributions will be valued. On the other hand, if I am being introduced to a company by an employee or an outside consultant, I know I need to do whatever I can to bond with the owners, as quickly as possible. Naturally, all of this must be done with the utmost care and respect – every person wants his or her job to be mission critical and secure, not merely someone who can be stepped over. Also, no matter who makes the initial contact with me, I always must understand that if they deem me unworthy for any reason, that gate is likely to close forever.

The key takeaway here is this: As a communications consultant, you are going to succeed or fail as a direct result of the person or people who engage with you on behalf of client companies. The "work" the company does is likely to provide the basis for your efforts … the subject matter of the communications efforts you will organize, distribute, and manage on their behalf. But the powers, talents, and whims of your liaison will either constrict your capabilities or allow them to soar.

This provides another angle reinforcing my appreciation for the McNeill PR Triangle: When I explain it to potential clients, I can emphasize the importance of their investments in ensuring our relationship is fruitful. I have had executive assistants and CEOs as my liaisons, and in those different scenarios, brilliant successes have been achieved. My best advice is to treat your main point of contact as a VIP, always endeavor to make them look like a superstar, and never miss any good opportunity to build your relationships with the company's top brass.

Small Companies, Up to Ten Employees

I am starting small for the obvious reason: Most likely, every potential aspect of communications consulting is going to apply to a company with a small staff, where the group must account for every nuance of operating the business.

Knowing the key skill set, the PR functions, bearing in mind the McNeill PR Triangle, and fully understanding the importance of time management – and your liaison – to your success, we can assess the small company's most likely needs against our primary functions.

I have worked with numerous companies of this size over the years. If my hourly costs were lower, I think I would probably still be working with most of them. However, since ongoing expenditures involving thousands of dollars create pressure for small businesses, I have seen many of these accounts play out relatively quickly, after taking this type of route.

Consistencies and Variations by Client Size

Table 4 Small Company Consistencies and Variations

Analyst and Historian	Often the "origin" story is more succinct and the company's clear leader(s) is already front and center. The company's history and its present are also at the forefront, and key client developments demand attention.
Strategist and CCO	After learning about the company's history and its most pressing new developments, prepare to be "hands on" on all marketing channels in aligning messaging and measuring results moving forward.
Patron of Sales	The essential ingredients of how the company is winning business, and otherwise setting itself apart in its community or sector, are the rocket fuel for marketing purposes.
Patron of Customer Service	Also of great use in marketing are the processes, people and other innovations the company is using to create value for its clients.
Relationship Developer	Especially where social media is being used as part of the marketing mix, cultivating and harvesting leads from those activities can justify the entire PR budget.
Storyteller	It's likely that most of the external writing will be up to you, although it might also largely be rewriting. For stories for the media and possibly for owned media channels, endeavor to find the best ones and bring them to the world.
Marketing Maven	There's also a good chance that no one else is giving a lot of thought to strategic marketing. As you engage with the media, helping to deftly explore advertising opportunities is shrewd. All knowledge you can bring to bear on paid media – and sponsorships, which often involve trade-out opportunities – where increasing traffic, inquiries, and/or sales are potential upsides, adds incredible value.

1. Homework and planning to build up to the launch or the big news story.
2. Announce the launch or the big news story.
3. Plan further news releases around major projects and campaigns to deliver a steady flow of strategic content to the company's owned media channels.
4. Measure and assess efforts against budget.
5. Back to step 1 and repeat.

I have always enjoyed this type of challenge and seen solid results in using my talents to impact small businesses. When a single client win or loss can make or break the entire business, the application of Darnell's Law can lead to a sustained need for PR services, or alternatively, the reassignment of those funds to some other aspect of the business, like paying the rent.

Medium-Sized Companies, 11–100 Employees

The leap from a small to a medium-sized company is massive. The business that grows to the point of having a staff of ten or more people possesses a vast amount of practical knowledge, and often, the leadership consists of several individuals, each of whom is vital to ongoing success. These added dimensions can increase the complexity of addressing communications challenges, especially depending upon the level of support they are given from company leaders. Here is a sample discussion that may apply to what you encounter with a business of this scale.

Compared with smaller companies, my track record for building lasting relationships with companies of this size is significantly better; still, every business is different, and the changes that come from one day to the next can make it, break it, or make it a better or a worse scenario for a communications consultant. To the example I provided for a sample handling routine for a small business, I am adding a few elements here, which are more likely to come into play.

1. Expect to regularly have more research to do and keep up with. Also, be ready for planning to be necessary on an ongoing basis. At any time, there are bound to be multiple "big news stories" in the pipeline, and other marketing activities to track and possibly contribute to. Everything is subject to change, and flexibility is the key to becoming an asset over time.
2. Be prepared to serve as the "news bureau" to package stories and relevant media assets; to provide media relations expertise; and to present (and potentially cross-promote) the best results on the company's owned and social media channels, and in other communications activities, such as newsletters.
3. Plan further news releases around major projects and campaigns to deliver a steady flow of strategic content to the company's owned and social media channels – and communicate that information with other stakeholders in the company to help everyone understand what will be happening over time.

Table 5 Medium-Sized Company Consistencies and Variations

Analyst and Historian	Compared to the very small company, the backstory is even more focused on the products and/or services currently being offered and the most valuable client relationships – but also, personnel.
Strategist and CCO	While the early going is likely to reveal company history and top developments, it may be harder to learn about marketing activities. Therefore, the communications functions may need to operate within specific boundaries ("silos") that can change over time.
Patron of Sales	In the best-case scenario, there is an open door to the sales leader and they know that your efforts will produce vital fuel for them.
Patron of Customer Service	Those who maintain the client relationships are often unsung heroes – you can be their savior and champion if you can illuminate their importance in the company's success.
Relationship Developer	Depending on factors like who is handling social media, how much direct contact you have with key clients, and how much access you have to information from those types of activities, there is great potential for you to impact your client here.
Storyteller	Most likely, writing and rewriting efforts will be your primary function, and applications will abound. Finding the right priorities and the most beneficial ways to use your talents will be essential.
Marketing Maven	As with a smaller business, if you are handling media relations, you are bound to be a primary conduit for advertising and sponsorship opportunities. Even considering advertising can impact earned media results, so finding ways to deftly interface between your client's marketers and media opportunities is well advised, in line with the company's marketing budget.

4. Measure and assess efforts against budget.
5. Back to step 1 and repeat.

Engaging with clients of this size is well advised, especially when you are given priority access to the company's leaders and you can engage them in your activities and your reporting processes. Such companies are not immune to being shaken up by the economy or by winning or losing big accounts. However, if you can establish yourself with the organization as the means for getting its best stories out into the world, you are likely to earn a lot of love.

Bigger Companies, 100+ Employees

This is another situation where the size of the client organization is going to have a huge impact on your roles. Within the organization, someone will have the authority to oversee communications, and this could be an executive position like CEO, CMO, Managing Director, or perhaps a partner with broad authority. Your liaison will either be that person, or work for them. I have a few specific examples to draw from for organizations of this size: Crest Digital (150 employees), Cutters Studios (200+ employees), and my U.S. Air Force Reserve unit (1,500 members). Respectively, my duties in each of those scenarios went from having a wider to a narrower focus.

When I was hired by Crest Digital's Executive Vice President of Sales and Marketing John Walker, that was a full-time position as the company's Marketing/Public Relations Executive. It was the first time the growing company ever had anyone handling PR ... and in the beginning, the owners were not big fans. Perhaps it is the case that smaller companies are more inclined to think of using PR practices to set themselves apart – but the issue can also be cultural or based on other factors. Misunderstandings about PR are commonplace. In the span of ten months on the staff at Crest, I was able to generate media coverage around many of its core strengths in different fields, while also helping to generate buzz in top-tier trade publications like *Variety* and *The Hollywood Reporter*.

Cutters Studios brought me onboard as a PR specialist, where Managing Director, Partner, and now President Craig Duncan made it clear he would manage our agenda, which was necessary for an organization with multiple offices and interrelated divisions. Handling the account with a healthy but tightly managed budget, we have had massive impacts on the company's success since 2014, while also putting certain practices in place to maximize efficiency. With Mr. Duncan running the show, we move quickly and address priority opportunities at a very sophisticated level.

My experience as a Public Affairs Representative for my Tactical Fighter Wing in the U.S. Air Force Reserve focused exclusively on my squadron – and more specifically, on a small field of developments that led to assignments from Lt. Colonel Bobby D'Angelo, who oversaw Public Affairs. While attending college and serving as a reservist, I volunteered in this position,

Table 6 Bigger Company Consistencies and Variations

Analyst and Historian	If given the opportunity to research this company's history, consider yourself lucky, and move fast. You will probably need to jump right into tactical initiatives very soon, requiring you to learn on the job.
Strategist and CCO	Addressing the marching orders provided by your lead(s) is your recipe for success. Completing the very specific mission(s) put before you will hopefully have the desired impact, and if so, you are more likely to be given more scope and resources in the future.
Patron of Sales	It may be enough to be aware of the company's sales activities – but also, you may be going very deep in this field, or for one or more projects. If so, count on your performance to be highly scrutinized.
Patron of Customer Service	As with your connection to sales, you will be wise to take stock of the company's product and service offerings as time allows. What you learn is likely to bear on the results you are able to achieve, which might be a formidable challenge. If so, be prepared to make the case as to how much value there is for the company in what you're learning and sharing.
Relationship Developer	The most vital relationships you develop with larger organizations are probably going to skew toward internal ones. You may be responsible for connecting and uniting individuals who might not know each other's best strengths or vulnerabilities.
Storyteller	Be ready to tackle whatever writing assignments are put in front of you with passion and style. Seeking to take a lead role in the organization's communications activities is bound to lead you in the right directions.
Marketing Maven	If you are a maestro who is up-to-speed on all things related to marketing – especially digital marketing – that is probably going to be your entrée into an organization of this size. If you are more of a writer with less marketing knowledge and experience, it may take some time before your work opens doors among the marketers.

wound up getting some training in photojournalism, and having some opportunities to contribute photos and stories to our squadron's newsletter.

Here is the type of formula that may apply to your activities on behalf of a larger organization.

1. Your mission is going to be based on the application of one of your primary skill sets ... or maybe, two or more of them. Expect your role to be limited, while understanding it will need to meet all standards.
2. Creating something that is reflective of the organization's values, culture, and tone will be of grave importance, while also fulfilling the objectives of your liaison or commissioner.
3. Given the opportunity to provide more of the "news bureau" functionality discussed for smaller organizations, you can potentially expand your mission to ensure your work reaches wider audiences within the organization and beyond, depending upon the objectives of your liaison.
4. Once your project is completed and carried through distribution, taking the initiative to plan follow-on projects of importance to your liaison and/or others within the organization can present multiple opportunities.
5. Otherwise, it is wise to measure and assess your efforts against expectations and the budget, and to proceed according to what you learn.

In the big picture, it may not prove to be essential to determine the perfect size for a communications consulting client. Forging ahead in this field, you will learn about opportunities through research or contacts, and as they arise, you must pursue them in ways that appeal to your experience, interests, and needs. Still, analyzing the various client scenarios according to company sizes is bound to pay dividends, sooner or later. While it is no big surprise to imagine having more scope and freedom in a smaller company, and having a more specialized and focused role, your familiarity with the need to shape-shift and/or "right size" your efforts will allow you to prepare for whatever comes your way.

Exploration

1. What key benefits do you anticipate receiving from working with an organization with more than 200 employees?
2. Based on your career experience to date, what company size do you feel it would be best to work for in the immediate future, and why?
3. Do some research to discover employment opportunities for communications consultants in your area; list one or more of them with the size of the company behind it.
4. Now, change the location for your employment opportunity search to two different places you could imagine yourself living. List one or more of them with the size of the company behind it.

5. Describe a scenario where your liaison has little experience, but you have no exposure to executives at higher levels. How do you make the most of it?
6. How can you ensure you have the experience and skills to establish yourself as a specialist in the field of communications consulting, but also continue to learn more about integrated marketing, so you can grow into bigger opportunities?
7. Can you identify two or more specializations that are complementary – where increasing your expertise in one also improves the other(s)? What are they?
8. Imagine you are hired as a communications consultant, by a middle-level manager at a company with 20 employees. After a month, you meet the owner for the first time. What do you tell him/her about yourself?
9. Now, imagine it is the Fortune 500 company CEO you are meeting, and you have been working for the manager in a field office for a month. How do you introduce yourself in that case?
10. Explain how "Darnell's Law" applies to a situation in your career where you received terrible news.

14
Media and Its Usage

This section illuminates the job of the communications consultant in the big picture. As we walk through the main facets of this profession and see how it all works together, it is time for us to explore media and its usage. As history has shown, social networks can come and go, but if you have the knowledge and ability to manage images, video, and audio, and use them as staples of your storytelling, you will be in great shape to succeed.[1]

I often tell my clients that an image can make a story … and by the time I am done handling any project that gets a lot of traction, everyone understands my obsession over high-quality visual elements. Of course, I had this focus in my work long before the birth of Instagram. It is not just about photos, graphics, and illustrations, either; from media outlets to businesses to individuals looking to set themselves apart, there is a rising emphasis on the creative use of video … and that goes for audio as well, whether as music or in the form of podcasts.

Images

In 1992, I found myself "starting over" in my career and needing to find a job. From the Orlando Sentinel's classifieds, I answered an ad from a video production company seeking a producer. Very soon, I was spending my days there in an odd world that may someday be the setting for a novel. This company with Vietnamese owners had pieced together quite a business, but its gear was mostly purchased at auctions, leaving it a little short of state-of-the-art. For one project, my client had used one of our systems to compile the rough edit – called an "offline" version – for their video. Typically, when the different systems speak to each other, the Edit Decision List (EDL) data from the offline can be imported into the more sophisticated systems used to compile a finished project in the form of an "online" edit. Unfortunately, our two systems were not speaking to each other, and this was a problem I

DOI: 10.4324/9781003177951-14

was left to resolve. The Internet was mostly a "message board" back then. By sleuthing around and applying some ingenuity, I was able to translate the EDL so it could be read by our online system. Based on my Century III writing experiences, I saw this as an editorial opportunity, and after writing the story and pitching it to editor Brian McKernan at *Videography* magazine, I had my first byline article (in other words, it credited yours truly as who it was written by) accepted for a national publication. Right away, Mr. McKernan asked me, "So what are you thinking of for images?"

Even though I was a big fan of beautiful cinematic imagery, I still was not yet especially proficient in creating it. After shooting a roll of film in whatever camera I had, one frame did the trick, earning this caption: "The author with his elusive EDL." That experience taught me that no story is complete without pictures… which eventually became, "an image can make a story."

There is an article on my blog entitled "Story Pictures" (https://up.darnell works.com/?p=1534), where the subject is Marko Costanza, a renowned artist in the realm of sound creation and recording for the entertainment industry. The picture shows Mr. Costanza in t-shirt, shorts, socks, and a pair of classy high-heel women's shoes, with a microphone pointed down at his moving feet. The background presents a highly organized arsenal of yard implements and other noise-making paraphernalia. Together with the headline "The Sound of Violence" and some more expertly presented prose, the package scored photographer Gus Powell and writer Joel Meares a feature in the *WIRED* magazine. If you use Google's image search for Marko Costanza, you will see many similar images showing him at work, which have appeared in countless prominent media outlets. Often, these stories allude to the fact that few people know his name, while many people know his work. To me, this remains a sterling example of how imagery provides the essential ingredient in generating interest in a story. Without having great images to include in these story packages, I feel they would be far less impactful, leaving the talented Mr. Costanza even more obscure.

- Further evidence of how I have applied this diligence in consistently employing vibrant imagery on behalf of my clients can be seen in these visual timeline case studies: http://bit.ly/DWAvtip

There are good reasons why I am linking the importance of images to the role of a communications consultant and showcasing an example from the pages of *WIRED*. In my opinion, most of the executives who would hire someone like us would be convinced enough by this example to admit, "Yes, that's what we had in mind when we hired you: We want to be in *WIRED*."

This provides a shortcut, allowing us to make a case, like so: To get what you want, we need great images.

Establishing that prerequisite for generating excellent media exposure is necessary, because even with support from the top, getting images in the right specifications (or "specs") can still be incredibly difficult. So, when it comes to working on any story for a client, it is now drilled into my approach to begin talking with them about images at the beginning, and diligently continuing to seek them out until I get something suitable. Even when I start with this request, the last things I am awaiting are usually the images.

Typically, the communications consultant needs to resolve the image quest in such a way that the results are in the form of high-resolution photography which, if used in a print media publication, will be sharp and clear. While the specifications for publications can vary widely, a good rule of thumb I have come to rely on for specs is to be able to provide JPEG images saved at the highest quality setting, that are at least 1,000 pixels wide on the longest side and are 300 "dots" or "pixels"-per-inch in resolution. Thankfully, most smartphones can capture photos at a quality that exceeds those standards, depending upon the settings. If the file itself is above one megabyte in size, it will probably work fine for non-print publication. Also, images are almost never too large, although you are going to want to become as adept as possible at editing digital images. Adding that to your skill set will allow you to take whatever you can gather, and then prepare and provide it to various media outlets according to their specific needs.

- You will find a great introduction to photo editing here, courtesy of Wikipedia: https://en.wikipedia.org/wiki/Image_editing

Image Production and Sourcing

Where do these essential storytelling assets come from? First, let's establish that you have a VIP role in discussing and using them, and therefore, in how they will come to exist. With that in mind, consider making the case to commission a professional photographer – if you feel you can do so without jeopardizing yourself. To help you explore this pathway, check out this article from Ginger Makela Riker, entitled "How to Find and Work with a Professional Photographer": http://bit.ly/FotPro.[2] In that story, Ms. Riker shows a broad range of professional photographs while also explaining how and why it is necessary to find the right fit with a pro, while also being prepared to discuss budget. This is a situation where most likely, the old cliché of "you get what you pay for" will apply – if you have done your homework in evaluating the project, the photographer, and every other aspect of the mission. Sounds high risk, right? That is one of the reasons why you might have to make another choice in how you go about getting your images.

Is there a key project participant who has taken photos already, or who you can convince to capture something for PR usage? If so, this may be your best option. However, if these photo assets are dated or have been used in the past, those details can adversely impact their value. Alternatively, if the project is visual in nature, using its imagery (book cover, poster, frame(s) from the video, early sketches, etc.) is another possibility.

The idea of finding a "stock" image that will work well for your story may seem somewhat unlikely, and until recently, going that route was often relatively expensive as well. However, offerings from the current world of stock photography may perfectly suit your needs. With the proliferation of powerful cameras and expanding ranks of photographers of all skill levels, the major stock image libraries continue to swell with every type of image imaginable, where most are searchable to the finest degree. By following this link, you will find a solid listing of some of the world's top stock photo galleries, which you can use to explore your image quest and research costs for various images, all at no expense (to be clear, there is usually a cost for using them, but not for searching them out).

- Top Stock Photography Libraries via Creativebloq: http://bit.ly/18stock

Several years ago, I signed up for something called the Dollar Photo Club. It was based on a monthly fee, and by paying that, one could download any of the images in the vast archive for any type of use, where no further royalties were due to the photographer. Dollar Photo Club has folded, but as you can see on this link, its main premise lives on in new ventures.

- Best Dollar Photo Club Alternative via woorkup: http://bit.ly/BdpcA9

And if you would rather just search through a massive, growing database of high-quality photographs that are free to use with zero costs, be sure to visit http://www.unsplash.com. Should you find yourself unable to resolve your challenge through any of these approaches, getting a good image may come down to you.

We could spend a lot of time discussing what it takes to capture quality images that can qualify as "story pictures." This is an area where the rise of Instagram provides a shortcut; if you are not already using it, I suggest you set up an account right away, or at least visit the site and use it to scan through

Communications Consulting

the infinite flow of imagery representing modern-day visual storytelling in the hands of individuals and every type of organization. Because Instagram images can easily be embedded in other websites, deft use of this service can help address the dilemma of providing imagery to accompany stories. Keep the "originals" for photos you use on Instagram in case you get requests for them ... but in the meantime, consider becoming adept in the use of this tool as an effective strategy for leveraging the power of imagery. This short video from *Outside* magazine highlights the basics: http://bit.ly/MaGram.[3]

While this discussion has focused on photographs – obviously, using illustrations and infographics can also creatively address the visual aspects of your storytelling objectives. Behance.net is one of the top websites you can access for free to search for illustrations and the artists behind them.

Videos

For the foreseeable future, we can count on having and relying upon multiple networked devices and using them to access a great deal of live and recorded video content.[4] Technology is racing forward to give us increasing speeds and to make Wi-Fi more widely available, and most of us are using that to access more video. Beyond the endless entertainment available on Amazon Prime, Hulu, Netflix, YouTube and TikTok, brands are also delivering video content on their websites and social media channels to drive significant interactions with their audiences. According to international research from Brightcove and Vanson Bourne, only one out of five people does not use social media for brand engagement or feel that video is the best way to research a company. By late 2016, brand videos were driving purchases for most U.S. consumers.[5]

Here, I simply want to substantiate the value of video in communications efforts and talk through a few main types, while providing some great examples. In my career as a press agent serving high-profile companies in the creative industries, my job has often come down to promoting a video. This started with coordinating network promos for NBC's seaQuest TV series before moving on to promos for Disney Channel and other TV networks, and then, international commercials, music videos, TV and film main title sequences, and full rebranding campaigns for TV networks. Each of these types of video projects is relatively distinct, and promoting them for news value involves specific research and diligence. Continuing to enter new doorways as they have opened, I have embraced more and more opportunities to apply my skill sets to the needs of phenomenal storytellers creating different types of video content. If you follow this link, you can learn much more about what I broadly refer to as Promo Videos.

- Promo Video Primer: 30 First-Class Examples – https://up.darnellworks.com/?p=4724

To me, that blog post represents some of my best work: It is highly informative, and it also provides rich insights that can be used readily. Chances are, any professional who is thinking about marketing at a high level can go through that material and find something from the promo, case study and behind-the-scenes video discussions that inspires their own inner storyteller. As mentioned in the article, most of those videos were designed for business audiences, yet the creators made efforts to ensure they appeal to almost anyone.

Taking these examples to heart, think about the videos you might launch into the world. Whether you follow in the footsteps of Chris Do or Sunny Lenarduzzi in producing educational videos (https://www.youtube.com/c/thefuturishere and https://www.youtube.com/SunnyLenarduzzi), Sam Jones in producing interviews (https://www.youtube.com/theoffcamerashow), The Katydids in producing an original comedy series (https://www.youtube.com/thekatydids), or any other uniquely personal calling, video content is clearly a substantial means for reaching and connecting with audiences.

Audio

Think about all the ways we can listen to radio, music, and other recorded audio content, and you can instantly understand our human dependence upon the sonic spectrum. My own children are rarely free of some source of audio information pouring into their ears. We have already established the rising role of video on the center-stage of our attention spans, but the case for audio may be even stronger. Perhaps because we can listen while we drive or do just about anything else, and because with even the simplest radio device most of us can pull unlimited audio entertainment right out of the air, this format of content is the very definition of the word, omnipresent.

For more than 40 years, the U.S. National Public Radio program "A Prairie Home Companion" has reached listeners across the country through their ears, artfully demonstrating the medium's capacity for magic which relies upon viewers to conjure the visual spectacles based on soundscapes that challenge – and sometimes defy – imaginations. As we approach 100 years of reliance upon the type of entertainment, we have become addicted to thanks to our records, cassettes, CDs, and radio broadcasts, our computers and digital devices demand more and more content as we roam from sunrise back to our bedrooms, day after day. Podcasts are now mainstream, and so is the regular coverage reporting on the best new podcasts in every niche of subject matter.

The trends of digitalization and automation are also increasing the importance of audio as a means of interacting with the world through our devices. Referred to as Voice User Interfaces and supercharged with artificial intelligence, we know them as Alexa, Siri, Cortana, Google Assistant, or the little microphone icon in our phones' messaging and search apps. They are the smart, computerized voices we are talking and listening to more and more, thanks to the carousel of progress.

Video and Audio Editing, Production and Sourcing

Earlier in this chapter, assessing the challenges of producing and sourcing images took several forms. After introducing the subject of image editing, the conversation turned to sourcing ... where suggestions were made about enlisting outside professionals, seeking solutions among project partners, and exploring stock options, all based on project particulars, including budget. Next came a brief discussion on the creation of photographic images.

Editing video and audio is at least a little more complicated than editing individual images, requiring more robust hardware and more complicated software. Still, Google and YouTube have answers and tutorials for just about everything, and learning to find solutions to problems is extremely important for communications consultants. Those are good reasons for me avoiding in-depth guidance on editing, but here is another: You may not need to be a video or audio production expert to succeed in this job. In fact, it may suffice for you to be able to wrangle the video or audio assets you will use.

With that in mind, here are some specs I use for requesting video assets when I am working on a project.

- Specs for PR Video: 720p QuickTime/H264 or MP4/approximately one megabyte per second or less.
- Notes: QuickTime is Apple's video format, and "H264 or MP4" denote the commonly used MPEG-4 video compression standard. "720p" is the size dimension, which breaks down as 1,280 pixels wide by 720 pixels high. And "one megabyte per second or less" lets my clients know that, for example, a 30-second video file should be encoded to render it 30 megabytes or smaller in size.

Over time, video specifications have continuously changed, and the evolution continues. For the foreseeable future, if you have video assets that meet or exceed the above specs, you should be able to put them to good use.

- Specs for PR Audio: Stereo MP3s recorded at 16- or 24-bit sample size and 44.1 or 48 kHz sample rate, with a bitrate above 64 kbps.
- Notes: MP3 remains fairly standard, and addressing the fine details provided will generally ensure you will be able to use these files widely as communications assets. WAV files are of even higher quality, so starting with those will produce even better results.

While you may not need to be able to create video or audio content in most cases, you should be able to help distribute it. However, going back to how we approached resolving your image quests, you may indeed need to commission video or audio production, source stock options, or produce original content. Here are a handful of links where you can find valuable guidance and get your wheels turning toward solutions.

- Key Elements to Consider when Developing a Video – http://bit.ly/VidKeys
- wikiHow to Make a YouTube Video – https://www.wikihow.com/Make-a-YouTube-Video
- How to Make Videos for Business: Content Strategy – https://youtu.be/d8U01W3DIG0
- How to Make Videos with your Phone – https://youtu.be/j685NaMDVYE
- How to create a powerful podcast when you have no idea what you are doing – http://bit.ly/PodPowR
- Start a Podcast Now. Here's How. – https://www.entrepreneur.com/article/282282

Video and Audio Distribution

For individuals and businesses, the options for getting your audiovisual content out to the world in ways that allow others to engage with it (comment, like, share, etc.) are growing exponentially, even if you are not a celebrity, a major studio, or a broadcast network.

Personal and business videos can be posted for the world to see and interact with them on YouTube, Vimeo, Facebook, Instagram, LinkedIn, Periscope, Snapchat, TikTok, and Twitter, for starters. I list YouTube and Vimeo first because I have become accustomed to using those platforms as my primary means for distributing video content. When you post on either, you can easily share or embed your videos on other social media channels. If your content is a feature-length or short film (narrative or documentary), you have the option of submitting it to the likes of Amazon, Hulu, iTunes, or Netflix. I have seen many filmmakers offer their original film and video productions for sale on Vimeo.

Communications Consulting

In the world of commercial production, many times my clients in the creative industry are creating content that is for a brand and/or an agency. The brands pay for the usage rights, which extend from the actors' performances through to the music and the content. Addressing copyright issues is of the utmost importance in the distribution of video and audio content, especially if you are selling it (or earning revenue through enabling advertising to run with it, as YouTube allows you to do). My rule of thumb is, if you do not own the rights and you want to post it on YouTube, you need to clarify who the rights holders are, even if you just add a line like so:

> All rights reserved by the copyright holders.

The same rights issues apply to Vimeo, but I have seen that platform used widely by creative industry companies which create content for others, including brands, musical performers, and other agencies and business entities. Based on this experience, I typically counsel my clients to share their clients' YouTube videos for news distribution purposes, and to use Vimeo for their own promotions. With videos mastered on one or both of those platforms, we share those links with our media friends when the project is newsworthy (it is brand new, it has won an award, or it is topical for some other reason), and we tend to stick with using the Vimeo versions on company websites, knowing that when the rights expire, YouTube videos are most likely to go dark. We also use YouTube and Vimeo videos on other social media channels to increase exposure for the clients and the work.

When it comes to sharing audio content, you can also use YouTube and Vimeo to share those types of projects, but you will want to add an image to serve as the video content. Rights are always an issue in sharing audiovisual content, which is why you will need to explore licensing any music you use, and nail down the copyright matters related to your content.

For those who create original music and audio content, there are also specific platforms and distribution opportunities to coincide with the multitude of listening opportunities we turn to every day. A self-distribution platform for audio content that is comparable to YouTube and Vimeo is Soundcloud; like its video peers, users can offer their work for sale and otherwise control its use. For music and podcasts, many people think first of Apple, which offers this in-depth guide for submitting content and making it available to the masses.

- Working with Apple Services: https://www.apple.com/working-with-apple-services/

Bandcamp, Pandora, Spotify and others provide even more ready paths leading to audio publishing success of the highest order.

Distribution of video and audio content can represent top-tier media strategies on their own, and I have had the opportunity to work with filmmakers, musicians and artists who have gone from promoting themselves through their own channels, to earning distribution in theaters, on television and on all the major streaming platforms. Looking back on each of those success stories, they all leveraged shrewd, intelligent storytelling and high-quality media assets to engage with individuals and communities, where each step was essential to achieving the desired results.

Exploration

1. From your own experiences, name a business story that pertains to a local business or someone you know, and describe the photo(s) that accompanied it. If no photo ran with that story, what would be the ideal photo to accompany it?
2. List an example of a story that might use an illustration for its visual – and one where it might be best to include a short, looping animation.
3. Book a session with a local photographer to shoot your professional photo. This can be for your family or you and your significant other, but be sure to have one made for your use on social media. Make note of the business matters presented by the photographer regarding cost, usage, etc.
4. Think of a place you would like to go and perhaps write about, then visit both https://www.flickr.com and https://unsplash.com to research images you could use to accompany that story. What are the differences in using an image from Unsplash versus one from Flickr?
5. If you do not already have an Instagram account, set one up for your professional use as a communications consultant. Find something that represents your interests and post it there, then find me there (@RKDarnell), follow my account, and send me the link to your latest image.
6. From all the sources of videos listed in this chapter, list a video that most appeals to your inner storyteller, and two others, and explain what is most meaningful to you for each one.
7. Here is a link I have compiled where you can see some videos that have gone viral: http://bit.ly/VIRvid. From your own point of view or research, name three characteristics of videos that go viral.
8. List one idea for a web series that you might produce drawing from your personal interests – and another drawing from your professional interests.

Is there one that would cover both personal and professional interests at the same time?
9. Name a web series that is also a podcast, a magazine, and a photo shoot, which also appears on television. (Hint: It is produced by my friend Sam Jones – be sure to visit https://offcamera.com to fully experience Sam's brilliance in conceptualizing this project and bringing it to life as a career-building and dream-fulfilling exercise).
10. Thinking across all the ways to leverage the proliferation of media, and given a limited number of hours to reach the largest target audience for a client, where would you focus your efforts?

Notes

1 The Modern Marketing Dilemma and The State of Business Video. (2017, October). *Magisto.com.* https://www.magisto.com/video-market-size.
2 Makela Riker, G. (2016, February 18). How to Find and Work with a Professional Photographer. *Medium.com.* http://bit.ly/FotPro.
3 How to Master Instagram. (2017, February 17). *Outside.com.* http://bit.ly/MaGram.
4 Lunden, I. (2017, June 8). Cisco: IP traffic shoots Up to 3 Zettabytes by 2021, Video Will Be 80% of it. *TechCrunch.com.* http://tcrn.ch/2sj5vjB.
5 Brightcove, Inc. (2016, November 15). Three in Four Consumers Link Social Video Viewing to Purchasing Decisions. http://ow.ly/cFmv306fVQ7.

15
My Version and Your Version

When we began this discussion, I shared my general perception that there are individuals and businesses in the world that can benefit from having communications consultants in their life, constantly focusing on applying solid promotional communications principles on their behalf. Combining intelligent strategic thinking with that type of proficient diligence, our clients can reasonably expect to enjoy new opportunities to succeed in business. Mindfully adjusting the strategies and tactics as we go, applying solid management and customer service efforts can often sustain the productivity of the relationships and keep them on track for long stretches of time.

When I left the security of full-time employment 20 years ago, I was banking on the viability of these ideas with every fiber of my being. Considering how this training might enable exciting new career opportunities for you, I am equally giddy with excitement, anticipation and even a little bit of fear. After all, there is no reward that comes without risk.

Arriving at this section of the book focusing on the communications consultant in practice, here are the primary aspects of the "world-class skill set" that will guide your success: Account Management; Customer Service; Planning; Writing; Media Relations; Measurement; Reporting. Let's also review these other vital points we have explored.

- Many people think of PR as reputation management: I agree completely.
- Landing clients has required me to convincingly demonstrate that I am the best person to help them tell their mission-essential stories and present viable means for getting them out into the world, primarily through shrewd promotional marketing and earned media coverage.
- My primary business strategy since 2000 has been to position myself as a spectacular communications consultant capable of generating monumental results, and then to continually validate my skills and qualifications.

DOI: 10.4324/9781003177951-15

- Working at The Terpin Group (TTG), I honed each step necessary to consistently place stories in targeted, high-profile media outlets. Those steps are strategic planning, research, relationship-building with journalists and influencers, pitching, promoting and client relations.
- Ongoing PR success also involves understanding how PR functions apply to overall business operations and all other aspects of marketing.
- Today's leading marketing experts consistently point to a focus on building and maintaining positive customer relationships as the key strategy for dealing with change.
- One way or another, it is going to be up to you to significantly contribute to a company's success, so you have a lead role in deciding the correct course of action to accomplish that.
- Through this training and your diligence pursuing the assignments, you have prepared yourself to serve in these PR functions for your clients: Analyst and Historian; Strategist and Chief Communications Officer; Patron of Sales; Patron of Customer Service; Relationship Developer; Storyteller; Marketing Maven.
- Recalling the McNeill PR Triangle, in any client relationship, you are likely to succeed or fail as a direct result of your liaison(s). Simultaneously, whenever possible, you need to build your relationship with the company's owners.
- Most often, the subject matter of the communications efforts you will organize, distribute, and manage on behalf of a client draws from the company's work, its methodologies, the unique styles and philosophies of its leaders, and the status of its business developments.
- Social networks can come and go, but if you have the knowledge and ability to manage images, video, and audio, and use them as staples of your storytelling, you will be in great shape to succeed.
- Artificial intelligence, machine learning, and automation are already beginning to reshape work and the workforce. Fortunately for us, the communications skill set represents knowledge and abilities that can leverage these developments to drive higher productivity and economic growth for you and your clients.

Most days of the week, most times of year, you will find me at my desk doing the work I am describing here and making myself available to my clients based on their present needs. Managing my time is of the essence, so I have come to rely on various tools to keep myself on track, and to help me navigate the large and small efforts necessary to produce positive results for each client. In my follow-up book, *The Communications Consultant's Master Plan*, you will learn more about PR client services, the specifics of agency business, and what I call the PR master toolset. Meanwhile, the book you are reading is designed to give you a solid foundation and share many hard-earned secrets, leading you to become reputable and proficient in the field of communications, and highly adept in providing value to your clients' businesses.

When I was at TTG, I was one of eight account executives in the Los Angeles office. Many days we would begin with a quick meeting in the conference room, where we would go around the table and briefly talk about what was happening that day for each of us. Hearing about the dialogues underway with so many top-tier members of the media around the world was fascinating, as was hearing my colleagues describe the unique challenges they were attempting to solve, which put their talents to the test. Our General Manager Mike Garfinkel had his abilities tested as well: He had to match the interests and capabilities of each of his account pros with the needs of the firm's clients. To me, it is a safe bet that the results of any given account would be different in the hands of a different account person. That is the point I want to illuminate for you.

Having completed the chapter on personal brands and branding, you should have an excellent understanding of what makes you tick: Your interests, and who might benefit most from the application of your talents. Through the chapter Explorations, you have identified competitors in your area. By looking at the companies they represent (probably listed on their websites), you might have found one that piques your interest, either as a potential client for you or as a company that represents a niche you find compelling.

I can easily rattle off over a dozen different people I know who operate their own business as a freelance communications consultant. I am certain they all held full-time jobs at some time in their lives, and that those experiences are factors in their reputations and their confidence applying their skill sets for their clients. To see the full width of the communications consulting spectrum, try searching for "communications consultant" in any given city.

Such professionals represent unique sets of experiences and circumstances, and the specifics of their businesses are bound to function at least somewhat differently compared with the others. Where they are based, whether the proprietors are actively engaged with their clients on a full- or part-time basis, or whether they have more than one client, most likely the variations are much greater than the similarities. Still, each of them has figured out much if not all the subject matter presented in this book. As you advance, you too can establish your own enterprise; you have already been exposed to many of the most valuable lessons.

Entering early adulthood, my mother gave me a thoughtful gift. It was one of those engraved items sold in malls across America: a small bar of metal etched with the words, "What would you attempt to do if you knew you could not fail?" To be honest, the question vexed me. I knew I could fail, and to get where I wanted to be, I had a lot of work ahead of me that was not exactly what I wanted to do. I already understood that failure abounds. That mindset is where I started, but still, I became conscious of the vision of life I was shooting for, where I was more in charge, well rewarded for my work, and able to enjoy some security while also being able to provide that for my family.

It has been a privilege for me to come to work for my own company – my own clients – every day. I hope you will soon have the same pride and be able to experience the same rewards in pursuing your vision as a communications consultant. Moving forward, let these ideas I attribute to the Dalai Lama guide you forward.[1]

- When you understand your potential and are willing to embrace it confidently, you can absolutely make the world a better place.

Exploration

1. List five benefits that a business might receive by working with a communications consultant.
2. For the business in your answer to item one, list five different benefits it might receive by continuing to work with the communications consultant for longer than a year.
3. To become a communications consultant, what are the greatest risks you face?
4. What are the greatest rewards in store if you can establish your career in this way?
5. Describe three ways you can establish your capability to generate monumental results.
6. Imagine a scenario where you help place a story for an individual or a business (your client) in a media outlet. Describe the story and the steps you will take to see the project through. How much time will it take you?
7. When the efforts you describe in item six play out, what will you counsel your client to do with the story to generate more exposure or further address their objectives? How much time will you spend making those recommendations and helping to put them into action?
8. Achieving the feat you have imagined in the above two items will serve you well if people understand your role in making it happen. Think

about encapsulating the experience in simple case study format (Problem; Approach; Results).
9. Find at least five websites for communications consultants and look for their case studies where they explain how they have approached various problems for their clients and come up with solutions that validate their capabilities.
10. Now, go back to items 6–8 and complete those steps (it is okay if you are the "client") to get a story placed, to use it promotionally, and to organize a case study about the project. Repeat this loop until you are ready to sell yourself as a communications consultant.

Note

1 Lama, D. (2010, March 28). With the Realization of Ones Own Life Potential [Comment on page "His Holiness the Dalai Lama"]. *Facebook*. http://bit.ly/can_do.

16
Is Consulting Right for You?

There is a famous passage attributed to American mythologist, writer, and lecturer Joseph Campbell, where he makes a case for the benefits available when we follow our bliss. Poetically, he suggests this approach will lead to opportunities that are open to you alone.[1] Reading further into the introduction of this provocative theme at the website for The Joseph Campbell Foundation, we learn that adopting the concept requires more than just doing what we like. Indeed, Mr. Campbell encouraged us to fully commit ourselves to those things we are truly passionate about, as a means for fulfilling our potential and maximizing our contributions to our communities.

This broader perspective is illuminating when we consider some career advice which is popular, and yet, not necessarily very practical. You are probably familiar with the idea that if we do what we love, the money will follow… or in other words, that we should follow our passions. Yes, knowing one's passion is a key to happiness, but when it comes to building a career on solid ground, there may be more to the equation. That is why you will find endless references stating that following one's passions is terrible career advice. Personally, I still encourage you to stick to the path of self-discovery, and to regularly assess your status in the present, map out your vision for the future, make time to work on plans, goals, and dreams, seek out objective feedback, and apply it to your life. In the personal branding exercise you completed, identifying target audiences, and creating value for them became a focal point. Those are essential areas we must account for to ensure that following passions can lead to success.

As you determine how you want to focus your career, if there is no money to be made in your chosen realm, many will say you have chosen unwisely. Perhaps being poor but fulfilled in our work is the highest calling of all, but I feel there is a case to be made for finding a way to use one's talents to live at a standard that is personally fulfilling. With that in mind, rather than focusing exclusively on your passion at first, many successful executives emphasize

DOI: 10.4324/9781003177951-16

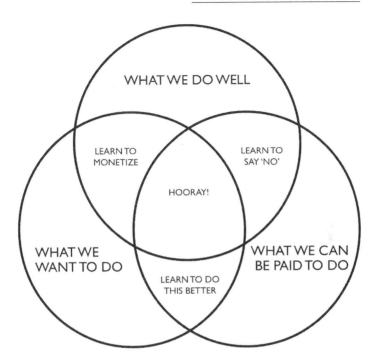

Figure 7 Happiness at Work.

doing what you are good at.[2] This illustration from Bud Caddell elegantly presents a surer means for pursuing an ideal career.[3]

Chris Dessi is an accomplished business executive, author, and speaker. In a 2016 article, he shared Steiner Sports' CEO Brandon Steiner's prerequisites for determining a person's optimal career plan. While passion is important, it should only be considered after completing a sound assessment, making a solid plan, then committing to accomplishing that plan, one step at a time.[4] That formula pulls everything together for me. I have seen many examples of people just following their passion to a bitter end, so I can completely relate to the points made by J. Maureen Henderson in this story.

- Three Reasons Following Your Passion Will Send You to The Poorhouse – http://bit.ly/PASSpoor[5]

I previously referenced a *Time* magazine article by Marty Nemko that pointed out these key aspects of job satisfaction, endorsed by thousands of interview subjects: Work that is not too hard or too easy; work that feels worthy and ethical; a boss that treats you well; coworkers you enjoy; moderate opportunities for learning; reasonable work hours; reasonable pay; reasonable benefits; job security; a reasonable commute.[6]

When you analyze those attributes in any field of employment, it is much easier to see why simply following one's passion in the early stages may be short-sighted. The wiser approach is to know where you want to wind up, learn the requirements to get there, and commit to making progress and taking steps that will lead you toward your destination over time. Also, remember that in many ways, the journey is the destination, so reassessing along the way may lead you in some new direction, toward some previously unforeseen objective or passion. To me, that is the beauty of life, and I would add, it is the potential prize in store for those who follow their bliss.

This chapter is here to help you assess whether launching a consulting business is the best choice. Since this is an especially important business decision, I want to help you understand some of the practical, financial, and legal matters that apply to the various choices. Let us begin by assuming you are on the verge of launching a consulting business that will soon take life, with roots in the field of communications.

The Making of a Communications Consultant

There is an incredibly smart way of distilling your essential identity while also embracing what distinguishes you as a leader – all from the point of view of the values you offer others. The term for what I am describing here is your Leadership Brand, a subject that co-authors Norm Smallwood and Dave Ulrich wrote a book about in 2007. Thankfully, in partnership with *Harvard Business Review*, Mr. Smallwood also published a handy, five-step guide we all can use to hone in on ours, and you can find it here: https://up.darnellworks.com/?p=77. Following this guidance, here is the latest version of what I have come up with for myself.

- "I want to be known for being thoroughly diplomatic, and proactively inventive, thoughtful and effective, so that I can be a source of savvy communications counsel for anyone I meet."

When I first discovered Mr. Smallwood's article, my agency was already going strong. While I did not yet understand how such a statement fit, the words "fame and fortune" have always summed up my ambitions, to a large extent. As you contemplate your leadership brand, retracing the steps that led me to mine may be relevant.

A powerful confluence of personal communications developments occurred for me in 1989. While hustling as a freelancer and a "temp" in Orlando and attending classes at UCF, I recall making the decision to really pursue my passions – more specifically, to assert myself more fully according to my interests – both in my Air Force Reserve unit and in school. By this time, I had already removed myself from full-time salaried employment. When I was freelancing for U.S. $10 per hour, of course I had no benefits, but also, my wages had no taxes withheld ... meaning I was responsible for paying the U.S. government at tax time.

By pursuing my professional opportunities as a freelancer and with the described personal focus, I wound up volunteering as my Reserve squadron's Public Affairs Representative, which proved to be extremely rewarding. In school, I revived a film-oriented student association, and as its president, I spent the next two years working alongside some incredibly talented people with similar interests to establish an exciting group initiative that generated all sorts of awesome opportunities for us all. That required me to actively communicate with a growing number of people by phone and prepare written communications that I submitted into *The Central Florida Future* student newspaper and published in newsletters. Encouraged by those efforts, I started writing a weekly humor column for *The Future*, which later earned a Scripps Howard Foundation Fellowship for me – while also helping me find my voice as a writer and get priceless feedback on my writing from faculty members and students. Those were some amazing doors that opened due to following my bliss! My goal in sharing this is to let you see how I had faced the problems of a moderately uninspiring job as a Reservist, and an academic progression that required much less than I had to offer. Listening to my inner voice and acting when I felt compelled, I made those leaps.

To graduate in my chosen field, I had to embrace the freelancer lifestyle ... which meant that by age 24, I was constantly networking and looking for jobs, primarily in the film industry. The implications of one of those gigs proved seismic. A friend told me about a freelance writing job for the massive Century III (C3) post-production operation at Universal Studios Florida. When I interviewed with VP of Sales Pamela Tuscany (now VP-GM Production at Universal Studios Florida Production Group), I was offered U.S. $200 to write six press releases per month. Together with Ms. Tuscany, we devised a system that worked like a charm: I made a form based on the Copy Platform, and Ms. Tuscany asked her Account Executives to complete one apiece for their biggest projects each month. She then reviewed the submissions and chose her six favorites, which she handed me. From there, it was up to me to prepare a press release for each one.

Through that amazing experience, I was relied upon to write about developments ranging from investments in new technologies to the company's detailed, high-tech contributions to blockbuster movies, massive commercial productions, and live television events. While the pay was humble, the opportunities to learn and grow were through the roof. Ms. Tuscany took my stories and put them to use in ways I was left to imagine; in other words, I did not handle media relations on behalf of C3. However, I did discover that there were "trade media outlets" covering the relevant industries, and saw that one or more might take interest in C3's latest investment or client solution, especially if the company also placed an ad.

At that time, I still did not see how my future business writing endeavors had been given a foundation. In school, I had been more interested in arts and literature, and my own mother had toiled away for many years as an extremely gifted poet, whose way with words delighted and inspired me as much as any of the songs I grew up hearing. My aspiration was to be a great writer, and that meant following in the footsteps of Ernest Hemingway, Edgar Allen Poe, or Mark Twain, for a few examples. Perhaps I should have paid more attention to the fact that each of those revered writers had long since passed.

To propel my career forward, I wrote poetry like mad, I painstakingly researched publications that might publish them using the encyclopedic annual Writers Market books ... noting the submission requirements and the endless "pet peeves" cited for each choosy gatekeeper identified. Wave after wave of keenly polished submissions went out, resulting occasionally in a photocopied rejection slip. Eventually, a few surreal human exchanges occurred, and to this day, I recall the positive and the negative responses. To my eternal delight, I even scored a handful of publications that went beyond the "vanity press."

Here again, I uncovered an unforeseen benefit: From the bottomless investment I poured into becoming a published poet, I earned a solid education in media relations. Lessons learned? First and foremost, every gatekeeper demands deep familiarity with their publication and audience. Also, they almost always want something that is exclusive, and whatever you send needs to be new and/or newsworthy.

Time marched onward for me and increasingly, my interests in computers, writing and production led in more profitable directions. By writing nonfiction stories for film and TV industry trades, I scored more ink, and my first story in the internationally distributed *Videography* magazine even came with a U.S. $200 paycheck.

In 1998, I was appointed as the marketing and public relations executive at Crest National Hollywood Labs, a family-owned business with a long, successful history as a film lab, a broadcast post-production company, and an optical media manufacturing and fulfillment operation. The matriarch still drove herself to work most days, navigating her Bentley from Beverly Hills through the gate of our cavernous parking garage. Whenever we crossed paths, she eyed me suspiciously. She and her husband had built their company over 50 years without a PR person, so why did they need one now? Well, I proved my value starting very quickly, writing press releases about various developments in the company that generated ink far and wide. I also helped establish sponsorship relationships with many film festivals and represented Crest at events from Southern California to Park City, Utah. My legacy, however, was building the company's first website, where the entire world could learn about the company, and see the face of Jean Stein along with her other directors. For that, I managed to earn her esteem.

Having proven my value as a staff communications executive with a post-production company, drawing on my background and expertise, there were three steps remaining to prepare me to relaunch as a consultant. My friend Tim Street hired me away from Crest in 1999 to serve as marketing director for his production company that specialized in network TV "promos." There, I also was charged with helping to lead the company into commercial production. As I learned, that was a very tough nut to crack.

Thanks to Mr. Street, I was introduced to several aspects of the TV industry I never knew existed ... where TV shows and networks are promoted to viewers – and even specifically to advertisers, agencies, and media buyers – for sales purposes. We all are familiar with movie trailers, which are related to this realm, but there are also many companies and executives I met through the PromaxBDA trade group (now PROMAX) who come from what was previously the standalone Broadcast Design Association (BDA). These are often small design companies focused on using graphic design and animation to help broadcast and Internet-based entities brand, package, and present themselves to their audiences. So, my time with The Spark Factory was an immersion into the creative industry as it applied to TV networks in Los Angeles ... a powerful draw for talents worldwide.

My next opportunity was with TTG, where I learned how to land clients and handle strategic communications needs primarily focused on reaching investors, consumers, and other businesses. Because TTG had successfully built its expertise in the high-tech marketplace through offices in LA, San Francisco, and New York, and because we were in the thick of the "dot-com" era where companies and their investors were throwing money at every legitimate (and some illegitimate) promotional opportunity, we had a steady stream of companies willing to spend about U.S. $10,000 per month to retain us.

As an employee, I managed to command almost U.S. $1,000 per week, with benefits.

When I was part of a three-person team that won a U.S. $20,000 per month account on my first day at TTG, I had stars in my eyes. Within my first 60 days, I also helped win two more U.S. $10,000 per month accounts, and for one of those, I managed almost every aspect of their relationship with the agency, including renewing them after the expiration of their initial contract. Returning to my takeaway from my experiences with C3 that were "through the roof," being part of a group of professionals that was pitching major business publications like the Associated Press, The Wall Street Journal, and The New York Times every day and placing stories for our clients felt surreal. It made me realize that if I did my homework for a given client, and if we could find the right angle, the potential for getting media exposure was unlimited … and importantly, that exposure was extremely valuable.

One day while making my commute down the 405 freeway in the normal bumper-to-bumper traffic that made the ten-mile drive last over an hour, I remember hearing a National Public Radio story about the good people of Puerto Rico, who were preparing for a hurricane. Of course, I was stuck in traffic headed to a job where I earned about 10% of what my clients were paying for my services, and I really had no passion at all for most of my clients. Still, it surprised me when I found myself wishing I was in Puerto Rico preparing for a hurricane. I knew it was just a foolish fantasy, but it was also a wake-up call.

Since closing the Florida-based Darnell Works, Inc. and moving to California, I had learned so much about the creative industry, about the business world at-large, the value of PR, and the means used by PR firms to attract, engage, and serve clients … and even how to handle relationships when the parties break up. Banking on that experience, I decided to stake a new claim as an independent communications consultant.

I turned 34 on my last day at TTG. Thanks to the kindness and support of Mike Terpin and Mike Garfinkel – who had the contractual right to tax all revenue I earned from their former clients for a full year but chose instead to simply wish me good luck – my income doubled the day I left.

Business and Tax Considerations

Someone once told me that a good accountant (or Certified Public Accountant, CPA) saves more than she costs, and since I never had a strong mastery of tax return filing on my own, I began taking that advice in 1988, after I started freelancing full-time. Over a span of more than 30 years, the accountants I have worked with have proven to be invaluable business partners, and in my experience, so long as you pay them to handle the filing of your annual tax return, their advice on other matters is usually "on the house." So, when it comes to finding the best structure for your business, knowing what types of expenses can and cannot be deducted, real estate matters that will affect your tax liability in a given year, insurance, and estate planning, I encourage you to seek out a CPA that comes highly recommended from others you trust. Of course, before engaging with them, it is perfectly fair game to ask for an estimate of their fees so you will know what to expect.

My first accountant was very professional with me even when I was making little money, advising me that when I started to make more, I would then want to incorporate. In the United States, business structures continue to evolve. Some of the more important issues are liability (whether you can personally be sued for matters related to your business), partnership, and then some other aspects having to do with recordkeeping and tax matters, which can vary from one state to another. Blake Stockton provides a very comprehensive overview comparing the options here:

- Best Small Business Structure: LLC vs. S Corp. vs. C Corp. & Others: http://bit.ly/BizStrux[7]

If you decide to start doing work on a freelance basis, where there are no taxes being withheld from what you are being paid, you are a sole proprietor, or an independent contractor. Although in rare circumstances those who are paying you may stipulate that you carry a certain amount of liability insurance or acknowledge that you are self-insured, there are often very few other requirements to operate a business in this way. As a sole proprietor, you may only need to secure a local license for your type of business (i.e., restaurant or construction permits, zoning or selling permits, etc.) and register your trade name (e.g., Mike's Auto Repairs) with the county clerk. At tax time, you will also need to file a tax return claiming your income, where you can report your itemized expenses against that income. Generally, you can also claim mileage for your business travel, meals, and any other legitimate expenses that represent your costs of doing business.

In the U.S.A., companies with more than one employee may also be required to carry Workers' Compensation Insurance. To see how this affects you, visit http://bit.ly/WCIlaws.[8]

In 1992, I had a small cash windfall based on having a screenplay optioned, so I followed my CPA's advice and relied on him to create and file the articles of incorporation for an "S" Corporation business called Darnell Works, Inc.

Florida had an annual corporation filing fee that was several hundred dollars, and I also had to maintain a current occupational license (now known as a Business Tax Receipt) through the Orange County tax office. This business had only one employee at that time, and it was used to invoice my clients at C3, the publications I wrote for, and the TV shows I worked on in Orlando. When we moved to LA in 1998, the money I had saved in the company bank account quickly dwindled, and since I did not know about the possibilities for working as a communications consultant covered by this book, I folded the corporation and focused on getting a job.

When I left TTG in 2000, I made the decision not to incorporate again, focusing instead on operating as a sole proprietor. Somehow, I was able to get a business banking account set up using DWA as a trade name, although it was not a straightforward process. Feeling that incorporating was overly cumbersome and complicated, I chose instead to spend extra money on taxes to streamline the process of doing business as a consultant. Was it the best decision? Clearly it was not, as I eventually figured out … but since we soon left California, it was not the worst decision, either.

Geographic Considerations

This discussion is meant to help you fathom the various means of handling a business from practical, legal and tax perspectives. Obviously, one of the most practical aspects has to do with a person's geographic location. In Los Angeles, having just left one of the world's best high-tech PR firms, I had a lot going for me. Where one lives and does business is not just a factor in how they are perceived, but naturally, it also determines the ease with which they can meet in person, as well as important factors like events and organizations they can easily participate in. Theoretically, however, by using the Internet, email and telephone, skilled communications consultants can consistently generate remarkable results from anywhere. In 2001, I put that theory to the test.

For us, the decision to leave LA that year had everything to do with family and quality of life. Beth and I were expecting our first child in August, and while we had loved the Southern California lifestyle when we were childless, we were not so excited about staying put for our next phase. Much of our family was still located in Illinois and Wisconsin, or 1,000 miles south between Tampa, Orlando, and Jacksonville. But right in the middle of that span, in the Blue Ridge Mountains of North Carolina, Beth's mom and stepdad had settled in and gotten busy flipping homes and building new ones from scratch. This attracted other dear ones, including Beth's grandmother as well as a sister and her family. In short, we purchased a lot and agreed to buy one of the new homes to be built, and we set our sights on a new life in the college town of Boone, where our little one could grow up around other little cousins and family members.

The year I spent operating DWA in LA was a blast. Certainly, I had a lot of positive momentum coming out of TTG, but being able to field opportunities as they arose in the City of Angels, it was the opposite of what I had experienced before landing the job with Crest National. One of the best advantages I had going for me was my friend Lisa Cleff-Kurtz, who continued referring me as a go-to PR pro while pursuing her own ambitious business opportunities. Also among my good fortunes was a lead to handle PR for a boutique visual effects (VFX) company in West Hollywood that was operated by the owners of Rock Paper Scissors (RPS), one of the commercial production industry's premier editorial operations. To this day, RPS continues to edit some of the most exciting commercials, music videos, and entertainment programming, without a great deal of self-promotional fanfare. Recognizing the need for its sibling VFX company a52 to have a wider reputation, I was engaged to handle PR, and the prolific relationship lasted more than a decade.

Through that situation, I connected with other very high-profile agencies and production entities known for innovation and hallmark standards in the global creative industry. Telling stories and showcasing advertising projects from the likes of a52, ATTIK, RPS, Tool of North America, and music company Endless Noise, I had gone full circle in handling PR for businesses – and come back to film and television production and post-production ... but with full creative-industry clout and perspective.

So, we loaded up our cats and our belongings, and traded LA for Boone. Doing everything possible to reassure my clients I would be returning for visits every few months – and that I was committed to continuing to do extraordinary work for them – I managed to retain an impressive roster of four companies. As the next phase kicked in, the pay I had been making in LA was cut in half, while Beth entered the Aunt Beth/Mommy era. For the next 14 years, much of her considerable energy went toward parenting, coordinating construction, and volunteering.

To operate my business in Boone, I procured a local occupational license, and since our California bank also had a local office, we were able to carry on with the sole-proprietorship approach. A couple of years into that, we met the extraordinary CPA we work with to this day. From the beginning, she heard me out on my idea for "keeping things simple" regarding not incorporating, but before long, she picked her moment to demonstrate to me how incorporating would save considerable money, and I followed her lead. In 2005, with the help of Jamie S. Leigh, CPA/PA, Darnell Works, Inc. returned to the USA's tax roll system as a North Carolina-based "S" Corporation. For her help managing tax matters including payroll with Ms. Leigh, and our insurance and retirement accounts, Beth also became an employee.

Leaving California was a giant leap of faith. For all I knew, sustaining the business would require us to move back – or elsewhere – before too long. My hope was that my dedication to my clients would cement our relationships, and I put it all on the line from one month to the next. Thankfully, my roster held intact and even grew at key times – for example, in 2003, when global creative agency ATTIK came onboard, and in 2004, when I added Post-Works New York. Having an excellent tax professional on our team allowed us to navigate the issues involved in doing business across state lines, while also taking advantage of tax breaks to fund our 401(k)-retirement plan as fully as possible from one year to the next.

I promised to help you explore the practical aspects of self-employment versus traditional full-time employment, and beyond the point I have made about state-to-state requirements for Workers' Compensation insurance, another critical piece has to do with health insurance. Since we are self-employed, we do not have easy access to group policies which could offer significant savings. Our research shopping around in California led us to choose Blue Cross Blue Shield (BCBS). When we moved to North Carolina two months before our child's due date, despite BCBS being in operation here as well, we lost our coverage, leading to us having to pay for all delivery costs out of pocket. Over time, we stuck with BCBS as the best option from an extremely limited field of choices, and when our son was born in 2003, another ridiculous stipulation led to us having to pay all expenses for his hospital delivery out of pocket as well. In short, we pay quite a bit in premiums in exchange for surprisingly few benefits, and I am not aware of any better options for the self-employed in the U.S.A. We hope things will improve over time. Meanwhile, this reality is another facet of doing business as an independent contractor.

It Is Time to Act

By hearing about my career journey and thinking about your own ideas for employment, I hope the practical aspects of being self-employed are coming into focus. By now, we have covered all the key building blocks for anyone aspiring to do well in any field of business. Through that process, I have also shared my personal journey, where in certain situations, I was ready and able to operate as an independent contractor or consultant – while in others, I felt compelled to seek full-time employment. At those critical times when I had to decide how I would go about making money, the combination of experience gained together with my confidence in operating as an independent contractor opened a new possibility that is still holding strong in maximizing my earning potential and my career opportunities. By now, I hope this knowledge has sunk in, and it is factoring into your career strategy.

You have developed your personal brand by thinking about how you can best provide value to others, and you have also spent time identifying the audience you intend to serve. Perhaps you are ready to file your business entity locally and begin soliciting business. If you are drawn to the field of communications, the homework you have already completed is sure to position you as someone who can begin using the key skill set to help others.

It is also possible that you are not feeling ready to launch your own business entity. In that case, your best focus may be on finding a mentor who can shepherd you through the next level of your journey, and this very well may be an employer. Remember that those you compete with to land a job are pouring every ounce of energy they can muster into winning those opportunities. If you choose that route, I encourage you to use everything you have learned to present yourself as the ideal candidate.

On the other hand, assuming you remain onboard and interested in becoming an expert communications consultant, I now invite you to step beyond the basics. In my companion book to this volume, we will delve further into the specifics of day-to-day activities in service of clients, where PR practices are mission-critical in achieving success.

Exploration

1. Among your heroes in life, can you make the case for how one of them "followed their bliss"? What did that look like at the beginning, middle, and later in their careers?
2. Do you agree that completing a sound assessment, making a solid plan, then committing to accomplishing that plan, one step at a time, are wise steps to take before steering toward your passion? Why or why not?
3. What are your top five factors for being satisfied with a job?
4. Track down Norm Smallwood's article about building a leadership brand, complete the exercise, and share your statement.

5. After reading about my journey in becoming a communications consultant, what are the main concerns you have about seeking work as an independent contractor?
6. What aspects of being a self-employed communications consultant are you most excited about?
7. For self-employment where you live, what permits, licenses and/or insurances are required to operate as a sole proprietor?
8. Search out at least three friends who are self-employed to see how they handle health insurance and learn more about their providers and premiums.
9. In your city or county, or in the largest city that is close to you, list three communications consultants (or agencies) who appear to specialize in an area that matches your interests.
10. For those entities identified in your answer to question nine, if you want to compete with them, summarize how you intend to do that in 300 words or less. Otherwise, consider presenting yourself to those firms and their competitors as a job applicant or as an intern, so you can learn on-the-job.

Notes

1 Campbell, J. (2019, April 28). *Follow Your Bliss*. Joseph Campbell Foundation. http://bit.ly/JCbliss.
2 Liu, B. (2015, October 26). Why "Follow Your Passion" Is the World's Worst Career Advice. *Inc.com*. http://bit.ly/2RhVSz2
3 Caddell, B. (2009, June 3). Happiness at Work, a Venn Diagram –. *What Consumes Me*. http://bit.ly/HappWork.
4 Dessi, C. (2016, January 14). Why Following Your Passion is a Mistake--And What to Do Instead. *Inc.com*. https://bit.ly/1mY9rzF.
5 Henderson, M.J. (2013, February 11). 3 Reasons Following Your Passion Will Send You to the Poorhouse. *Forbes*. http://bit.ly/PASSpoor.
6 Ibid. Nemko, M. (2014, October 13). Why Following Your Passion Is the Worst Kind of Career Advice. *Time*. http://bit.ly/TimeMNem.
7 Stockton, B. (2020, June 19). LLC vs S-corp vs C-corp: What Is the Best for Small Business? *Fit Small Business*. http://bit.ly/BizStrux.
8 Workers' Compensation Laws - State by State Comparison. (2017, June 7). National Federation of Independent Business. http://bit.ly/WCIlaws.

Index

Note: **Bold** page numbers refer to tables; *italic* page numbers refer to figures.

ADDIE Instructional Design Model 33
Advertising and Promotion: An Integrated Marketing Communications Perspective (George and Michael Belch) 27, 97
advertising-driven business model 99
Alpert, Kim 74
Alphabet Network 98
American Memorial Day 100
Analysis, Design, Development, Implementation, Evaluation (ADDIE) 32, 33, 43, 69
Arden, Paul: *It's Not How Good You Are, It's How Good You Want to Be* 41
Arnold, Dave 104
artificial intelligence 87, 146, 152
The Artist's Way (Cameron) 125
ATTIK 14, 15, 22, 52, 57, 62, 63, 74, 76, 77, 123, 166; assignments 72; brands by **73**; clients 71; and Scion 100–3
audio distribution 147–9
audio editing, production and sourcing 146–7
Augmented Reality app 102
Austin, Linda 93

Baer, Jay: "Youtility" 85
Baker, David C. 54, 68, 69, 78, 81, 83, 86; *Financial Management of a Marketing Firm* 110
Balanced Scorecard 62
"The Balanced Scorecard: Measures That Drive Performance" 60, 62

Barney, Jay: *The Management of Organizations* 60
Barr, Roseanne 98–100
BCBS *see* Blue Cross Blue Shield (BCBS)
BDA *see* Broadcast Design Association (BDA)
Belch, George 27, 28; *Advertising and Promotion: An Integrated Marketing Communications Perspective* 97
Belch, Michael 27, 28; *Advertising and Promotion: An Integrated Marketing Communications Perspective* 97
Bezos, Jeff 49
BIEN 74, 75
bigger companies 136–8, **137**
Bill, G. I. 24, 81
Blake Project 52
Blake Stockton 163
Blue Cross Blue Shield (BCBS) 166
bottom-line objectives 14, 29
Boy Scouts' law 17
"brand as possibility" 31
"The Brand Called You" 33
brand creation 35–7; and development 69
Brand Culture Workshop 52
brand development 32–5, 38, 44, 69
Brand Identity Now (Wiedemann) 72
Brand Positioning Workshops 52
brand values 91–3, 100, 102
Branson, Richard 49
Breakenridge, Deirdre 123, 129
Broadcast Design Association (BDA) 161

Index

"Building a Practically Useful Theory of Goal Setting and Task Motivation – A 35-Year Odyssey" 60
business and tax considerations 162–4
business brands and branding 67–8; brand creation and development 69; building brands from scratch 69–75; rebrands 75–8
business communications 3, 30
business development 21, 54; pull/inbound/permission/content marketing 85–7; sales 80–3; sales in marketing 83–5
business reputation 14

Caddell, Bud 157
Cameron, Julia: *The Artist's Way* 125
Campaign Messaging Plan *113*
Campbell, Joseph 156
Carnegie, Carnegie 14; *How to Win Friends and Influence People* 12, 13
Carson, Nick 40, 41
cash flow and project flow: navigating financial challenges 109–12; profitability as business objective 107–9; project flows 112–14
John D. and Catherine T. MacArthur Foundation 50
Chandler, Tracy 74
Cleese, John 21, 22
Cleff-Kurtz, Lisa 27, 81, 123, 124, 165
client size 122; bigger companies 136–8, **137**; liaisons 131–2; medium-sized companies 134–6, **135**; small companies 132–4, **133**; universal consistencies 129–31
Coleman, John: *Passion & Purpose: Stories from the Best and Brightest Young Business Leaders* 91
The Communications Consultant's Master Plan 152
communications initiatives 3
communications strategy 94; in business 27–9; in career planning 25–7; in education 25
consistencies and variations: bigger company **137**; medium-sized company **135**; small company **133**
constructive culture 51
Continuous Connected Customer Journey 61, 94, 97, 98

Control Over Nature 103
Copy Platform **36,** 37, 159
Costanza, Marko 141
Covert, Adrian 103
creativity: as business practice 21–2; in creative industry 19–21; exploration 22–3
"crisis communications" 11
crisis-management mode 62
"Crunching the Numbers" 108
Csikszentmihalyi, Mihaly 93
customer engagement technology 61
Customer Experiences (CX) 97
customer service 1, 3, 51, 60, 87, 109, 151; brand values 91–3; connecting to customers 94–5; engaging human resources 93–4; leaders' emphasis on CX 89–91
Cutters Studios 51, 52, 64, 136
CX *see* Customer Experiences (CX)

Dahl, Darren 108
Daly, Matt 104
D'Angelo, Bobby 136
Darnell's Law 131, 134
Darnell Works Agency (DWA) 7, 81, 84, 89, 120, 164; closer to home 123–6; relationship 121–3
Darnell Works, Inc. 35, 163
da Vinci, Leonardo 31
Davis, Ziff 77
Degan, Michael 78
Dentsu 52, 63, 71
The Design of Business (Martin) 52
design thinking 53–5
Dessi, Chris 157
Digital Kitchen (DK) 130
direct and digital marketing 98
DiSC style 35, 37
DK *see* Digital Kitchen (DK)
Dollar Photo Club 143
Duncan, Craig 136
DWA *see* Darnell Works Agency (DWA)
dynamic public relations 36, 59

Edit Decision List (EDL) data 140, 141
EDP *see* Energias de Portugal (EDP)
employee activities 3
Energias de Portugal (EDP) 75

Enns, Blair 81, 85–7, 92, 93; *Pricing Creativity* 54; *The Win without Pitching Manifesto* 54
ENVOY 69–70, 74

Fargo, Matt 108
Farmer, Tessa 103
Feliciano, Dan 60
Ferguson, Stacy Ann 38
Financial Management of a Marketing Firm (Baker) 110
Florida-based Darnell Works, Inc. 162
Frames of Mind: The Theory of Multiple Intelligence (Gardner) 34
From Selling to Co-Creating (Lemmens) 86

Gandhi, Mahatma 94
Gantt, H. L. 113
Gardner, Howard: *Frames of Mind: The Theory of Multiple Intelligence* 34
Garfinkel, Mike 24, 27, 153, 162
Gates, Bill and Melinda 49
Genuine Creativity 22
geographic considerations 164–6
Getzels, Jacob 93
"global creative agency" 14, 62, 63, 100, 123, 166
Godin, Seth 37
Gomez, Danielle 74
Gomez, Jose Sebastian 74
Goodson, Scott 67, 78
Greiner, Larry 56; Model Curve 56
Griffin, Ricky: *The Management of Organizations* 60
Guilford, J. P. 22

Hacker Noon (Kagansky) 68
Haden, Jeff 68
Härén, Fredrik: *The Idea Book* 22
Harris Poll Reputation Quotient 12
Hemingway, Ernest 160
Henderson, J. Maureen 157
The Hippocratic Oath 16
Hodgins, Brent 28
How to Win Friends and Influence People in the Digital Age (Carnegie) 12, 13
human beings: components of 90
human resources, engaging 93–4
Humes, James 13

Hung Le 74
Hutson, Chad 121, 124

The Idea Book (Härén) 22
IGN identity system 77
image production and sourcing 142–4
instructional systems design (ISD) 32, 38, 69
integrated advertising campaign 19, 75
integrated brilliance 104–5
integrated marketing 97; ATTIK and Scion 100–3; GEICO 98; integrated brilliance 104–5; ISAM 103–4; Roseanne 98–100
intelligent communications 2, 93
intelligent strategic thinking 1, 151
Internet-based entities 161
"Internet of Things" 70
ISD *see* instructional systems design (ISD)
It's Not How Good You Are, It's How Good You Want to Be (Arden) 41
ITT 81

Jaffe, Darren 64
Jeneski, Loretta 78
job satisfaction 93, 94, 126, 157
Jobs, Steve 49
The Joseph Campbell Foundation 156

Kagansky, Yonatan: *Hacker Noon* 68
Kaplan, Robert 60
Kickstarter pre-order campaign 70
Kiehner, Elizabeth 77
King, Martin Luther Jr. 68, 94
KPIs *see* key performance indicators (KPIs)

Lao Tzu 39
Latham, Gary 60
Laurence, Bethany K. 111
Laziridis, Mike 53
leadership and management 49–57
Leading through the Turn (Mitchell) 52
Leigh, Jamie S. 166
Lemmens, Régis: *From Selling to Co-Creating* 86
Lenarduzzi, Sunny 39
Leviathan 51, 56, 57, 74, 103, 104, 121–3
liaisons 131–2
life insurance policy 81
Lippincott 31, 32

Locke, Edwin 60
Lois, George 21, 22
Luci Creative 64

machine learning 152
Malkovich, John 32, 33, 41
The Management of Organizations (Barney & Griffin) 60
Managing the Professional Service Firm (Meister) 109
marketing consultancy 70
marketing tactics 82, 85
Marketing Week Article 84
Martin, Roger 53; *The Design of Business* (Martin) 52
Matz, Scott 77
McGuire, Tim 64
McKernan, Brian 141
McLuhan, Marshall: *The Medium is the Massage* 28
McNeill, Don 130
McNeill PR Triangle 130, 132, 152
Meares, Joel 141
media and its usage: audio 145–6; image production and sourcing 142–4; images 140–2; video and audio distribution 147–9; video and audio editing, production and sourcing 146–7; videos 144–5
The Medium is the Massage (McLuhan) 28
medium-sized companies 134–6, **135**
Meet Blossom 70
Meister, David H.: *Managing the Professional Service Firm* 109
Melvin, Stu 77
Meredith, Justin 12, 29, 77
Mirren Business Development 28
mission-critical imperatives 3
Mitchell, Elise 56, 63, 93; *Leading through the Turn* (Mitchell) 52
Monty Python 21
Morrison, Mike 32
Musk, Elon 49

Needham, Simon 22, 71, 72
Nemko, Marty 126, 127, 157
network television promotions 120
Ninja Tune 103, 104
Nonfiction Spots 78
"Nonfiction Unlimited (previously Nonfiction Spots)" 78
non-traditional campaign 112
non-traditional "cross-media" ad campaign 101
non-traditional marketing 101
non-traditional media practices 101
Norton, David 60

Obama, Barack and Michelle 49
objectives: objective-driven communications showcase 62–5; types of 59–62
objective-driven communications showcase 62–5
"Objectives Strategies Results" 59
O'Brien, Mark 86; *A Website That Works* 85
OpenText 61, 94
organizational leadership 24

Passion & Purpose: Stories from the Best and Brightest Young Business Leaders (Coleman) 91
Peralta, Ric 71, 123, 124
personal branding exercise 156
personal brands and branding 30–1; brand creation 35–7; brand development 32–5; design (objectives, strategies) 37–8; develop your key components 38–43; implement and evaluate 43–4
Peters, Tom 33
Pink, Daniel: *To Sell is Human* 80
Poe, Edgar Allen 160
Positioning, Objectives, Strategies, Tactics, Administration, and Results (POSTAR) 32, 43, 69
Powell, Gus 141
Power, J. D. 90
PR activities *see* public relations (PR) activities
"A Prairie Home Companion" 145
PR Champion 129; roles and responsibilities of *123*
PR Client Services activities 107
Pricing Creativity (Enns) 54
Project Management Triangle 112
PromaxBDA trade group (PROMAX) 161
Promotional Mix 97, 98, 100–2, 105
public relations (PR) activities 97

Index

pull marketing 85, 86
push marketing 85
Putting the Public Back in Public Relations (Solis) 129

Qualtrics XM Institute (QXMI) 89
Quiroz, Michael Angelo 105

ReCourses New Business Summit (NBS) 81
referrals and inbound inquiries 82
reputation management and ethics 11; anatomy of influencer 12–13; business reputation 14; commitments to the audience 13–14; ethics in business 16–17; ethics in life 16; ethics in your practice and mine 17; exploration 17–18
Resort Pool Management (RPM) 80
retainer engagements based on hourly rate 82
Ridings, Joel 39
Riker, Ginger Makela 142
Roberts, Ricardo 75
Rock Paper Scissors (RPS) 165
RPM *see* Resort Pool Management (RPM)

sales in marketing 83–5
"sales through service" 86
Sarofsky Corp. 20
Sarofsky, Erin 20
Scion 63, 71, 72, 100–3
Scordato, Brian 108
Scripps Howard Foundation Fellowship 159
Shapiro, Michael 64
Shaw, G. Scott 83, 87
Sheridan, Marcus 85, 86
Sinek, Simon 68
small companies 132–4, **133**
Smallwood, Norm 158
social media strategy and tactics *124*
social networks 42, 140, 152
sole-proprietorship approach 165
Solis, Brian: *Putting the Public Back in Public Relations* 129
Sommerville, James 71
"The Sound of Violence" 141
The Spark Factory 84, 161
Steiner, Brandon 157
Stein, Jean 161
Stewart, Potter 15

strategic problem-solving 28
strategy 24; in business, communications 27–9; in career planning, communications 25–7; in education, communications 25
Stringer, Andre 74
subscription-based streaming media platforms 99
Sullivan, Mike 24
Sun Tzu 50
Sutton, Chris 90

Terpin, Michael 24, 27, 84, 109, 110, 162
The Terpin Group (TTG) 7, 24, 27, 35–8, 152, 153, 161, 165
Tobin, Amon 51, 103
To Sell is Human (Pink) 80
"trade media outlets" 160
Travis, Will 71, 123, 124
TTG *see* The Terpin Group (TTG)
Tucker, Brad 64
TUI 84, 86
Twain, Mark 160

universal consistencies 129–31
Universal Studios Florida (USF) 6
U.S. Air Force scholarship 80
U.S.-based Government Employees Insurance Company (GEICO) 98
USF *see* Universal Studios Florida (USF)
"Using Your Positioning for More Reward, Impact, Control, and Fun" 81

VFX company a52 165
videos, media and its usage 144–5; and audio distribution 147–9; and audio editing, production and sourcing 146–7
visual identity system (VIS) 74, 77

Walker, John 84, 136
A Website That Works (O'Brien) 85
What Color is Your Parachute 13
White, Jason 74
Wiedemann, Julius: *Brand Identity Now* 72
Winfrey, Oprah 49
The Win without Pitching Manifesto (Enns) 54
"world-class skill set" 151

YouGov Brand Index 31
"Youtility" (Baer) 85

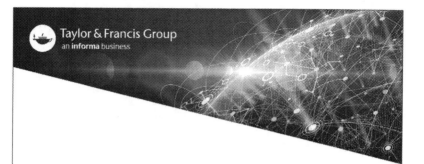

Printed in the United States
by Baker & Taylor Publisher Services